THE
RESILIENCE
TOOLKIT

Dr Alia Bojilova is a registered psychologist and former Lead Psychologist and Officer with the New Zealand Special Forces (SAS) with a specialty in resilience psychology.

She grew up in Eastern Europe during some of the most tumultuous times in recent history before immigrating to New Zealand at the age of 17.

While serving as a UN military observer in Syria, Alia negotiated her release and the release of her team after they were taken hostage.

Her PhD research identified the link between curiosity and resilience in the SAS. She has studied and explored resilience in some of the most testing and diverse contexts, including elite military teams, sports, entrepreneurship, leading global corporations, communities in duress, government agencies, the not-for-profit and the creative sector.

Since leaving the military, Alia has served as coach and advisor to leaders and teams globally and in New Zealand.

THE RESILIENCE TOOLKIT

Dr ALIA BOJILOVA

Originally published in New Zealand in 2023
by HarperCollins*Publishers* (New Zealand) Limited

First published as an ebook in Great Britain in 2023 by
Headline Home, an imprint of Headline Publishing Group

This edition published in Great Britain in 2024 by Headline Home,
an imprint of Headline Publishing Group

4

Cataloguing in Publication Data is available from the British Library

Trade paperback ISBN 978 1 0354 1546 5
eISBN 978 1 0354 1547 2

Cover design by HarperCollins Design Studio
Typeset in Arno Pro by Kelli Lonergan
Author photograph by Garth Badger, Thievery

Printed and bound in Great Britain by Clays Ltd, Elcograf S.p.A.

Headline's policy is to use papers that are natural, renewable and recyclable products
and made from wood grown in well-managed forests and other controlled sources.
The logging and manufacturing processes are expected to conform to the
environmental regulations of the country of origin.

HEADLINE PUBLISHING GROUP
An Hachette UK Company
Carmelite House
50 Victoria Embankment
London EC4Y 0DZ

The authorised representative in the EEA is Hachette Ireland, 8 Castlecourt
Centre, Dublin 15, D15 XTP3, Ireland (email: info@hbgi.ie)

www.headline.co.uk
www.hachette.co.uk

To my brilliant son, never stop seeking.

Contents

Introduction

Shhh – can you hear it? Turn down the distractions and listen. Your inner voice is whispering in your ears. Soon, these whispers will create a real outcome in your life. Whether you pay attention to them or not, these whispers will determine whether you hold still, fight, flee or freeze when life next presents you with challenges, and whether you become a mere observer, a passive participant or an active creator of your own life.

These alternatives are all about your resilience. Not the resilience you see in motivational posters or carefully chosen snapshots of other people's lives, but the sort of resilience that we need day to day as much as the pulse in our veins.

This book is about how you can harness your own resilience. It will show you how to get beyond basic recovery following a setback, and instead get to thriving: growing stronger and better than you were before your setback found you. This book is a pathway to helping you unearth and reframe fears so that you can unlock your potential.

Resilience is a necessity, a superpower that each of us can tap into given the right approach. Inside this book are the necessary tools to focus on what strengthens you and to reduce the impact of what might otherwise deplete you. They will help you make the most of opportunities and sustain your perseverance, energy and focus on pursuing better.

Over the course of my career I've discovered a four-step process that I consider the steps to resilience. These form the basic parts of the book: here you will broaden your **awareness**, deepen your sense of **belonging**, enhance your **curiosity** and activate your **drive**.

* * *

First, a bit about me. I am Dr Alia Bojilova. Like you, I am a complex map of many pieces. I am a mother, a wife, a retired soldier, a director, a partner in two companies – in New Zealand and globally – a coach, a psychologist, a mentor, a member of many communities, a friend and, importantly, a proud resilience geek.

I have studied and practised in the fields of psychology and peak performance for nearly 20 years. By sheer luck and an outrageous curiosity for life, I have worked along with, studied and supported some of the most remarkable heroes of resilience the world over. Each one of them is different at a glance, but they are all remarkably alike in that they adhere to the principles of resilience outlined in this book. These are people as diverse as special forces soldiers, elite athletes, remarkable leaders, entrepreneurs, movers and shapers of history and – most importantly – ordinary heroes, the likes of whom you might pass on the street today. In nurturing resilience, they have transformed the context of their lives from paralysing injury to strength, from poverty to riches, from deprivation to generosity, from loneliness to community, from aimless restlessness and ambivalence to purpose.

One of my most rewarding roles has been working with the New Zealand Special Forces (SAS) as a military officer and a lead psychologist. My role was to assist in selecting individuals and help them to sustain resilience as they operated in some of the world's most demanding conditions.

My SAS mentor used to say, 'Your most important job in life is to find your "thing". This is the thing that inspires and fuels you daily; that sees you contributing and carving the vision you have created for yourself so that it fuels and inspires others around you.' My 'thing' is resilience and I have obsessed over it for as long as I can remember.

A typical definition of resilience is 'the ability to bounce back following an untoward event'. This definition has always left me unsettled. An 'untoward event' according to whom? How long does it last? Who holds the criteria for resilience? Another question that has stirred my mind for some time is: 'What if the thing you are aiming to bounce back to is no longer there?' Bouncing back doesn't seem good enough.

It took time for me to realise that resilience is not necessarily about the 'bouncing back', or even forwards. Sometimes resilience is about your capacity to absorb and learn from your experience: to pause for a moment before you present your response.

The book that changed my life

Growing up in the Balkans presented me with plenty of opportunities to choose both the heroes and anti-heroes of resilience. I grew up listening to my father's stories of overcoming challenges – fears and bad habits – in pursuit of purpose, and was mesmerised by the power of his conviction and courage.

At the age of nine, I came upon a book about the life of a character called Victor. It illustrated the importance of resilience for me in a way that was unapologetic and confronting. The impression this book left on me shaped and influenced so much of my life and I think it would challenge you to look at life differently, too.

In it, Victor is lying in his small home somewhere in the Russian countryside. He's on his dying bed perched atop the stove – called 'poloti', a common setting in this context. In his final moments, Victor processes his life in vivid images. His experiences and choices rush past him as if he is watching a movie of himself. He recalls those events impartially, from a distance, as if he was never attached to them. Victor realises that he isn't struggling to part with his life. He finds there is no point in grieving for his life because he never really lived. I found this confronting. Had Victor chosen the road of least resistance?

A decade later, I came upon a different book written by a different Viktor from another part of the world. His perspective was entirely different to that first Victor. Unlike the first one, the second Viktor wasn't a fictional character but a real man. He was Viktor Frankl, a psychotherapist who wrote the book *Man's Search for Meaning*. His best-known quote is:

Between stimulus and response there is a space. In that space is our power to choose our response. In our response lies our growth and our freedom.

Frankl would challenge you to choose, to mind the space between 'the thinker and the thought'. As a holocaust survivor himself, he had the evidence to show that no matter your predicament, there is always something you can do to improve your situation. Even if that was to shift your perception and fuel hope.

I wondered, 'Would the story of the fictional Victor from Russia have been different if he had realised that he didn't just have to endure his predicaments? That he, too, had a choice regarding how to direct his life?'

In the years after I'd stumbled upon the fictional Victor and the very real Viktor Frankl, I discovered a way of holding at bay the anxiety of wasted life. Instead, I learned to hold the hope for a life of true meaning. By studying those who paved the way to resilience through their actions, I became committed to finding ways to turn seemingly insurmountable obstacles into stepping stones in an endless field of opportunities. In this book I am thrilled to share those tools with you.

The SAS

Around every corner, on every wall, in every room and on every block that combines to create the home of the SAS, there are remarkable stories of heroes that may never be told. Behind all those stories of heroism and extraordinary human effort lie ordinary faces, ordinary questions and ordinary challenges to which all of us can relate.

The motto of the SAS – a family of misfits, unrelenting dreamers, unwavering grunts and unlikely heroes – reads:

> We are the Pilgrims, master; we shall go
> Always a little further; it may be
> Beyond that last blue mountain
> barred with snow
> Across that angry or that glimmering sea,

White on a throne or guarded in a cave
There lies a prophet who can understand
Why men were born: but surely, we are brave,
Who take the Golden Road to Samarkand.

These are the words of James Elroy Flecker, who wrote 'The Golden Road to Samarkand' in 1913. Whatever Flecker's intended purpose or inspiration for writing those words is irrelevant here. What matters is the meaning they have taken on for SAS members and for me as a researcher, practitioner and storyteller.

For the SAS, these are the words of resilience in their purest form. They recognise that the most wicked of challenges are seldom imposed upon us but instead they lie within us. It is not about what happens to us, but how we engage with it.

The poem makes no promises of anything but challenge and soul-searching. It leaves no doubt that the journey will be unrelenting. Perhaps it gives a moment of encouragement, or perhaps it gives an even greater burden, but it tells us that our journey is entirely in our own hands, minds and hearts. The only real measure of resilience is whether we take that extra step on the road to our calling, the road to reaching our potential.

In my work with the SAS, it dawned on me that their resilience was made up of much the same stuff; there was an unmarked process to resilience that they all appeared to follow, albeit intuitively. The SAS context is shaped by tenets and values that are known and espoused by everyone within the team. Those tenets leave no room for personal derailers, or for the sort of doubt that leaves many of us stuck in inaction. Perhaps the magnitude of the threat, demand and risk that came from the 'outside world' was what made the 'inside world' of that team so focused on contributing to everyone's resilience within it. Resilience was a matter of survival.

However unique the SAS were, I was also about to discover that, no matter the environment in which it is tested, resilience appears to follow much the same process. Once seen, this process became so intuitive that my focus landed on gathering case studies and strategies to help make greater resilience accessible for more of us.

The ABCD of resilience

The following ABCD process is the True North to resilience, based on stories shared full-heartedly by my extraordinary yet remarkably ordinary research participants, volunteers, colleagues, friends, mentors and almost-tormentors-turned-teachers.

After my experiences in the military and the SAS, I explored resilience in peak-performance sport, global corporations, government, entrepreneurship, the arts, the not-for-profit sector and communities in duress. While the scope of my work broadened in ways I could not have dreamed, the process for gaining, maintaining and growing resilience appeared to remain much the same. However unique and diverse the resilience heroes I came across were, they all followed the same principles, consciously or unconsciously.

So what is it that allows some of us to recover, grow and even flourish after we experience setbacks while many others seem unable or unwilling to go on? The answer is simple.

Awareness

Belonging

Curiosity

Drive

This is the ABCD process that you, too, will follow through this book. Every step is essential. They are all incremental and each fuels the next.

The ABCD process is not linear, but a powerful, evolving loop that invites you to continuously grow and deepen your resilience.

Resilience is not a given or a trait, it is a series of decisions we can make so we can thrive in ways that matter to us. Resilience is fluid, not fixed. It is the result of the decisions we make on what and how we engage with, what and how we anticipate and commit to, what we choose to sit with, what we choose to discard and, most importantly, whether we choose to grow or reduce ourselves when we experience trials in our lives.

You are the only one who will bear witness to every moment of your life. While we can all learn ways to shape our lives intentionally, many of us permit the voices of our doubts rather than those of our hopes to shape our journey.

This book invites you to reflect, experiment, learn and apply principles that will see your resilience sustained and broadened. The evolving ABCD model means you will continuously be able to develop clearer awareness, deeper belonging, broader curiosity, and stronger drive – all the crucial elements required for you to thrive in change, ambiguity and unpredictability and move toward the vision that only you can conjure for yourself.

I am grateful that you, too, will get to hear the stories I have witnessed unfold in the lives of some of the most resilient people of our day – the resilience heroes.

Resilience is abundant in all of us. We all have the same ingredients for the mix that it takes to be resilient and thrive. Sometimes it is a matter of putting these in the right order and creating the right conditions.

PART 1
AWARENESS

1. Self-awareness

'Here it is – intimidating and glorious,' thinks Soldier H, 'the last bastion where the outcome depends entirely on the person who picks up the challenge.' He has made it to the SAS selection course after years of physical training, mental preparation and personal sacrifices.

Here, there will be no encouragement, criticism or direction from others. To drive him he will have to rely on his own steps counting down towards his goal.

The SAS instructors communicate only when they need to, and communication with other candidates on the course is strongly discouraged. The silence will only be broken by the sound of H's steps and his laboured breathing. No audience, no onlookers, no cheering or booing.

His sweat will blend with rain and swamp water. Every fibre of his body will be suspended in agonising tension for days. His feet will blister. The blisters will burst and his boots will dig deep into his flesh. His pack frame will rip into his hips and tear into his back. The pain will keep his mind awake and prevent him from taking the rest his body so desperately needs. He will become so used to the stench of his body and those of his mates that he will stop noticing it.

Every brutally blistering step of the way, his motivation will have to come from within. As intimidating as this selection course is, it is just a taster of the gruelling demands Soldier H will commit his life to *if* he is selected to serve with the SAS. To make it through, he has to remember that the pain and doubt he experiences are just temporary states and passing feelings. If he waits long enough without fully engaging in fear, they will pass.

As his energy is slipping away, he will have to make an ever-greater effort to stay focused on what matters and to make choices about what to lean on and what to dismiss. While there, he will hope for a second wind 100 times over.

This is a crucible event, a crucial moment in his life that will test, break or build H's resilience. Physical strength is important, but it pales in comparison to the levels of mental strength that will be demanded of him on the ruthless SAS course.

Soldier H scooped up every bit of advice he could to help him prepare. Having ticked off the obvious things – fitness, kit and navigation skills – one *big* thing remains: self-awareness. He will only have himself to rely on, so to make it through, he will have to select the thoughts that enable him and fight off the self-sabotaging ones.

It all sounds doable from the comfort of the couch, but can he really understand what pushing through this looks like?

How can he prepare for the levels of anguish, strain and discomfort that will layer up, day after day, hour after hour, in conditions he cannot even imagine?

His brain will try to outsmart him by minimising his dream of passing the selection course down to a fleeting idea, a dream to which he has naively committed so much of his life. His mind will conspire against him, making him rummage through his negative memories and doubts. It will cast the net of his imagination wide, forcing him to rethink any alternative possibilities he has considered for himself. His mind will flick through images of comfort, safety and prosperity – all things H will forsake if he joins the SAS.

His body will try to remind him of any physical weaknesses he has tried to ignore while training for this goal. Nagging pains will become deafening. His brain will try to protect Soldier H from making things worse for himself. The pain will cast his mind forward, warning him of the discomfort he will have to face if he stays the course. He knows no one has got out of this process completely unscathed.

The odds of his success are slim. There is no quota that the SAS aims to fill from each selection course. They can accept all or none of the candidates. Their selection criteria will not change.

The pre-selection process has already filtered out the best of the best candidates from the entire defence force. They have all dedicated years of their lives to training and preparation.

Yet, on average, fewer than 10 per cent of these top soldiers will pass the SAS selection course. If H fails, it will be best that he pulls the pin on his entire military career. His worst fear tells him that if he doesn't succeed, his current and only vision for life will be obliterated.

Serving in uniform is the only dream H has ever had. If he fails the SAS selection, his shame will be so great that it will reduce his scope for joy in any other military role. Anxiety kicks in – but H already knows that anxiety and fear can lie to him.

Soldier H will have to suspend or push past his self-doubt. It's easy to say but almost impossible to do. Self-doubt plagues all of us when there are no distractions or if we lack the discipline to combat it. It piles on quickly when we cannot offload it, especially when everything around us reminds us that we are one step away from losing it all. Most of us have lost something before. When we have, our brains quickly skip the recall queue, bringing back unresolved past experiences of failure and regret. H's only hope is that his aspirations will keep him one step ahead of his fear of failure.

One of H's mates had cautioned him: 'Don't leave the course unless they drag you out of it. Never volunteer yourself to withdraw. Everyone hears the same voices of doubt and fear in their heads. The difference is that those who make it don't act on those excuses. They keep going. To get to the end, I had to count to ten a thousand times a day!'

The voices of doubters have helped drive H to this point. But he knows proving himself to others will only get him so far. A fixed mindset will always find you out. H's SAS mentor, Sergeant P, once cautioned him: 'Proving others wrong may start you, but it will always eat away at you, and you will fail yourself in the end. If you try to tackle an important challenge from a negative standpoint, you have allowed the voices of your doubters to become your own. There is no escaping their impact unless your goal is deeply aligned with you, you know yourself and you can sustain a clear view of what it is you are moving towards, for yourself.'

H's only predictable company on the SAS selection course will be the gremlins on his shoulder: doubt, fear and pain. If he keeps himself in the right state of mind, these gremlins will become quieter and quieter, until they become inaudible.

Some moments can feel agonising, unbearable even, but H knows that if he keeps on keeping on, these moments will pass and, before he knows it, he will make it to the next moment. He will have something new to look forward to.

H thinks to himself, 'If you can make it through this minute, you can make it through them all, one moment at the time. Minutes always come one at a time, in days that come one at a time, in years that come one at a time.'

Observe your thoughts, but unless they aid you, do not become engulfed in them.

Two ways to resilience

There are two ways to resilience,
the right way and again.

There are never any shortcuts to replenishing or strengthening resilience. You cannot develop resilience by avoiding challenges or strain. To thrive and sustain our resilience, we need to observe and understand our emotions and thoughts and accept that they are fleeting moments in time.

Our states are not us and our emotions are not us, but we can become stuck in them if we don't pay attention. We are not our thoughts or feelings. If we get it right, we are the ones who witness them.

Resilience is an emergent thing. It only happens when we engage with our predicament, not when we avoid it. Resilience belongs in the process of striving towards becoming better than we were before, not in the outcome of every turn we take. It is a process. Resilience is the ability to push forward and persevere regardless of the obstacles you encounter, including your doubts.

In order to become resilient, self-awareness is key. Self-awareness is the ability to understand, select and direct your attention towards a goal. People might give it other names, but it always boils down to understanding your:

- strengths
- personal demons
- intent
- drivers.

SAS members develop their self-awareness by consciously working to understand what enables, drives and derails them. They look hard at their:

- powers
- shadows
- weak points
- fuel and sustenance
- anchor points.

To do this, they need to be open and ready to examine alternative ways of perceiving, engaging and responding (rather than just reacting) to what may otherwise be instinctive or in-built thought and emotional patterns. Sergeant P once told Soldier H that:

In trials, you can see when someone knows themselves and when they do, how they fully shape their outcomes by managing their thinking and responses.

We all have gremlins on our shoulders chatting away, nibbling at whatever motivation or hope we have left in our darkest moments. Their voices may change over time, but the only way to deal with them is by knowing how to engage with them. Soldier H knows his very well:

You become so familiar with the little voices in your head saying things like 'you won't make it', 'you're not good enough', 'you don't deserve this' and 'they think you're a fraud'. If you go ahead anyway, with each step you take towards your vision, these voices become quieter and quieter until they're irrelevant. If you learn how to manage yourself and drive yourself towards your goal, no matter how depleted you may feel, you'll grow from the voices of those gremlins rather than let them take over.

Those gremlins of doubt are brought on by fear. They are designed to protect us from pain and failure. They don't care about the goals we set for ourselves. They are concerned about minimising our risk of imminent pain and discomfort.

Soldier H has found that once the gremlins are under control, they can play a positive role: 'Many of the emotions that may otherwise paralyse or deplete your resources – like fear, shame and frustration – cease to be all-engulfing when you know yourself. These emotions can then serve as a trigger that focuses your attention more deliberately on what matters, on where your opportunities are and where your risks are. When you know yourself, you also learn to draw the line between perceived and real: past, possible and present.'

The best way to manage doubt and fear is not by fighting against them. By accepting their presence and making peace with their existence you will be better prepared to investigate them with objectivity. To get to this point, Soldier H asked himself some critical questions:

> What is it that this fear or doubt is trying to shelter me from?

> How do I redirect the blunt message it is sending me and turn it into an enabler for my success?

He then reminds himself that:

> Fear is just an indication that something matters, that something is shifting in me or in my environment. I can accept that. It reminds me to stand at my best, relocate my power, focus on my intent.

Awareness is the backbone of resilience. Self-awareness, interpersonal awareness and situational awareness all have tangible, immediate, long-lasting effects. Awareness had been the difference between life and death on more occasions than Soldier H and his team could count. It had become the backbone to their resilience as individuals and as a team.

Awareness makes us more effectively attuned to the shifts in our environment, better able to manage our resources and engage with the threats, challenges or opportunities in our lives.

For H, his awareness and resilience all started from the world he and his teammates nurtured within themselves. Self-awareness is what allowed them to step into testing situations with the readiness to shape or reframe their ways of thinking or their approach.

According to Soldier H, using your 'emotions to focus you rather than letting yourself get stuck in emotions' is key. The practice of observing your emotions and learning from them will grow your resilience with every encounter.

Tool: What's the matter?

Like Soldier H, we have all experienced fear, doubt and self-sabotaging thoughts. To examine yours, start the practice of unwrapping fears or doubts as nothing more than indications that something matters to you in this moment. Once you notice it, your only job is to take purposeful action to improve your odds for better outcomes.

Think of an example of a fear or doubt that currently depletes your resilience or obstructs you from your vision or your goals. Then ask yourself the questions Soldier H posed to himself:

1. What is this fear or doubt trying to shelter me from?

2. How can I turn it into an enabler for my success?

Examples of answers to these questions are:

1. My dream job has become available. This may be my only chance of getting it but I don't feel ready for it. My fear is that if I fail, my professional reputation and career will suffer. My fear and doubts are sheltering me from ruining my career.

2. Rather than holding back from this opportunity, I can accept my fear as a signal of how much this role matters to me. Rather than retreating, I will use my time to prepare. I will research the role, develop the skills I may need and carefully prepare for the interview. I will be transparent about how much importance the role has for me. This is a strength!

Once I get the role, I will commit to developing within it by proactively seeking mentors, upskilling on the job and outside of work hours and investing in the relationships that are essential for it.

Be where your feet are

Resilience requires deliberate actions done consistently.
Decades have passed since Soldier H participated in the
SAS selection course. Soldier H is trained to rely on and
perfect routines in every aspect of his military training and
preparation. Drills and routines are essential for survival
as a soldier. They are designed to help take control of what
may otherwise seem disorderly or overwhelming. Practised
frequently, they deliver the confidence to take on the unknown
with a clarity of intent.

Rituals and routines are just a vehicle and, as such, they can
take many forms and shapes. Soldier H has learned to seek
out and use whatever vehicle is most effective to get himself to
his intended destination; to select the mindset that will best
attune him to the intent he wishes to carry out. Every day,
he takes a moment of mindfulness, of connection with his
present, of paying respect to his current moment, no matter
what it contains. One of his mentors once coached him on the
importance of mindfulness in combat:

> To engage with your best, you have to be
> where your feet are.

In his time with the SAS, H learned that this rule means a
whole lot more than first meets the eye:

Engage with what is here and now, rather than with worry or rumination. If your mind wanders, you may miss your window to shape the situation in the direction of your will.

Be aware of what is at your disposal *now*. Do an honest inventory of your strengths, tools, gaps and vulnerabilities!

Wishful thinking will only get you so far – reality will find you out. Make yourself too small and your best way forward or out of your predicament will fly right past you. Worrying about the future or ruminating over the past can be defeating. As H says:

Could-a, would-a, should-a are so depleting. I have learned to take my lessons and move on with the added insights – good, bad or otherwise. Rumination and worry eat away at our resilience and you just cannot afford that.

Distraction could be fatal in combat context. Inability to be present in every moment of his current life, however, can take away from more than just Soldier H himself. His dearest. His family.

The power of grounding in the moment has never left H since he observed one of his colleagues demonstrate this ritual on a training exercise. The first time H witnessed this, the rain was pouring, and the humidity was off the charts. He was in the tropics in the height of summer. His sweat was mixing with raindrops, which provided a welcome relief from the scorching heat. He was about to enter the jungle.

H's colleague was new to the team, but he had mana – a presence that you can feel but no one could describe. He carried his mana with grace.

H's colleague took his shoes off and grounded himself with a prayer just before entering the jungle patch that was to be our home for the next week. He explained, 'I am not religious, but in my Māori tradition, you take your shoes and hats off before entering the wharenui (meeting house). You enter each new place with the awareness that you are about to transition between realms. You are leaving the outside world (where Tūmatauenga, the god of war, may reside) and entering a new world (where Rongo-mā-Tāne, the god of peace, may live). You enter each new space with utmost respect. Grounded in your strength and your intent, with open mind and heart.'

That ritual has remained and evolved with H. However busy his mind or strained his body, he takes a moment to ground himself as every new encounter deserves his respect, intention and openness.

H knows to 'be where his feet are' so well, the minute he tries to break this rule his body and brain send warning signals throughout his being. The physical endurance is easy. It's just mind over matter. But unless he maintains awareness, the tension in his eyes will come close to unbearable and his ears will begin ringing as if his receptors are setting the limits on his capacity to absorb his day. He has learned to push himself past his limits, and now he has to mind those limits carefully in order to be at his best.

Soldier H has learned that to create the most impactful results and thrive, he must conduct himself and his resources like a carefully orchestrated symphony. Unless he does, his ability to be present will be yanked back by memories of loss, grief, perceived failure, or of extraordinary feats of survival and adventure that provided him with endorphin saturation the likes of which his current life can never match.

To be resilient, you must give everything that matters full presence and attention. In order to do this, it's important not to spill the burdens of one day or experience into the next, thereby polluting the present or the future with what has been, rather than being open to the potential. In contrast, most of us start each new day as if the previous day has not ended. We spill over and repeat. We walk through new chapters of our lives without ever adding new meaningful content. Instead, we copy and paste, rinse and repeat. We simply don't notice the 'now' as we are too busy dragging the echo of yesterday around with us.

We are more than the subtotal of our past experiences. We are not our past but we control how we define it and what we will gain from it. We are more than our fears and our worries. We are in control of how we dispel them. Our resilience depends on whether we can engage with the present with intent while remaining open to the possibility that there is so much more to live for ahead.

Soldier H has proven himself. No one can question his resilience. But he is painfully aware that resilience sits close to grit, and his grit has nearly cost him his all. Self-reliance and grit can turn into detachment. His folders full of confronting experiences, more extreme than most can comprehend, can make him seem aloof, even arrogant. None of this is what he feels. He knows resilience demands the discipline of knowing when to be what and to whom.

Resilience is not a done and fixed thing. It demands continuous attention, but it always starts from the same place – self-awareness.

Tool: Your resilience markers

Take stock of your current resilience markers. There are two steps to this exercise:

1. Define what resilience means to you. You can write this, draw it, even sing it if you like, just as long as it uniquely represents your own definition of resilience.

> *To do this, consider your own hopes, needs and expectations of resilience.*
>
> *How will others know resilience when they see it in you?*
>
> *What does it look like when you think, feel and act resiliently?*

2. Describe the things that block the access ways to the resilience you aim to achieve. Answer the following questions in relation to the resilience you are aiming to achieve and sustain.

> *What am I doing that works against it?*
>
> *What am I not doing that works against it?*
>
> *What is in my way?*
>
> *What can I access to aid me in achieving this?*

I am asking you to commit to this activity now because no matter what you gain from this book, your version of resilience is unlikely to radically shift or change. Resilience shows us at our best. If it is to hold any value, this version of our best is deeply personal and subjective. Working through the pages of this book will give you:

- more scope to what you can achieve with your resilience
- a deeper understanding of what resilience does and what it takes
- increased access to resilience pathways
- a broadened resilience baseline that you can maintain with greater consistency.

What is awareness?

Awareness is the gate to resilience, no matter the challenge that lies ahead. Awareness in all its forms – self-awareness, situational awareness and awareness of others – is important. So important, in fact, that the word 'awareness' is thrown around all the time. You may have seen it listed as a part of the selection criteria for a job interview or heard it used as a source of criticism or praise, or as a judgement of presence or absence often linked with social fit.

Here's the thing – awareness is not a superficial nice-to-have in the context of resilience. It is an absolute necessity not just for surviving but for thriving.

Awareness is so important that SAS members described it as the gate to resilience. If you don't have it, you don't pass through trials and setbacks.

The gate to resilience

Self-awareness is a mindful consciousness of your presence, strengths and weaknesses, and the value and directions of your actions. Self-awareness requires having a clear perception of your mental and emotional states. Willing as we might be, that's a lot to ask of us.

If we are hopeful, we may think we can summon that clear perception on a good day. If we are realistic, we know that a myriad of biases, demands and distractions will get in the way of it. Whichever way we may be inclined, awareness is a non-negotiable foundation for resilience.

Strengths and spill-overs

Deep self-awareness involves recognising:

- how you can react to different situations in a way that amplifies your intended outcomes
- what triggers sub-optimal responses in you
- why you may feel the way you do toward certain individuals or situations
- how not to carry or spill-over from one situation to the next
- where your attitudes, beliefs and thoughts come from and how to locate the levers to change them, if they no longer prove fit
- how you relate and respond to others in a way that deepens trust and connection
- why others may perceive you in the way they do
- how to help change or comfortably sit with others' views if they seem incongruent with yours.

The list goes on and on, but the important part here in the context of resilience is that awareness gives you the *why* and *how* to the *what* and *who*.

In its simplest form, we think of self-awareness as knowing yourself in the moment. That means *how* you are, *why* you are the way you are, *how* you may need to be and *why* the gap.

The most common questions that spring to mind when thinking about self-awareness are the overused 'Who are you?' and 'How are you?'

These questions are flawed as measures of self-awareness. They can invite a myriad of responses and can be delivered in countless different ways – cross-culturally, cross-contextually, even at different points of the day depending on nuance.

Some of us may have readily available responses to these questions. It's the sort of stuff we dish out at the kinds of gathering that invite appropriate self-disclosure. Some may be able to go deeper with what we know or assume about ourselves – what we think we stand for and even why we stand for it; what we assume we are made of; what our strengths are and where they come from.

Most of us have a concept of how to describe ourselves using those indicators. Some of us may have no clue what to say, while others will have all the wrong answers. For many of us, our narrative for self is like a record on repeat and, often, it's not even the soundtrack we've selected for ourselves but one that has been played for us all along. These can come from our families and upbringings, our societal context, current or past experiences, misguided readings of who we are, even a poorly written line from a performance appraisal of a past boss we didn't even like, or a compliment we once perceived as verging on naive. They become the lyrics to the soundtrack of our lives.

In many cases, these lyrics grip our attention precisely because they are incongruent with who we feel we are. Yet we choose to listen to them long past their best-before date.

Many of us focus on who we think we were and who we ought to be rather than who we are in this moment. Going by an image of our best past self or casting our minds forward to our ultimate future self can be motivating, and this has a place in building resilience. But relying solely on this is a flawed approach to finding resilience. As one of my mentors would say, they are as 'useless as a flatscreen TV on a camping trip!'

To move forward, we need to accept who is standing there staring at us in the mirror and truly live by the principle of 'be where your feet are', with our eyes, minds and hearts open to the possibilities.

As my friend Dr Anita Sands says, self-awareness means no trimmings, no compliments, no ranks, no corner offices, no crutches. Awareness of the identity that's there to meet opportunities head on and heart full calls for the most important discipline we can ever pursue – that of employing unbridled curiosity and utmost openness to the question of 'Who it is that stands facing me in the mirror *today*?'

Awareness demands that we know who we are, not as it is contorted and propped up by the shades of our privilege or discomfort, but by the value and lessons extracted by us, the intimate awareness of the important person standing there, staring at you in the mirror. Not by what happened to you but how you grew through it.

This often demands deep dives, steep climbs and the right tools to take on the depth or altitude. If we get this right, awareness isn't static or fixed in time. It is an evolving exercise, an unflinching commitment to reading through and writing the pages of the most important book there is – yours.

To be of any use and to have a chance to see ourselves truly thriving in ambiguity, self-awareness needs to meet us where we are, with all that we have found in life. To be where our feet are today, in the readiness for what we are about to tackle, ready to deploy only what is most beneficial for our next step.

It is an exercise that – as the most resilient among us would warn – often requires us to break through layers of fog to find what is only ours to see. It also demands the fullness of knowledge of what underpins this vision – the values and motivations that define us, not as they have been imposed on us but as we have tested, fortified, questioned and strengthened through intentional engagement for ourselves. This is not a journey worth taking if it's not taken properly.

Tool: My personal 360

Most of us excel at acting like someone we are not and feeling something we don't feel. True resilience starts with an honest audit of where, who and how we are.

Do an honest inventory of your strengths, gaps, vulnerabilities and resources – the good, the bad and the ugly.

Where or who you are today may not reflect the whole of who you are. It certainly will not contain the whole of who you may become. After all, we are always evolving.

MY PERSONAL 360°

1. In what situations do I think I am at my best?

4. What can I do to be at my best more often?

2. What seems to be predictable about me?

5. What is one thing, if I could change it, that would help me most?

3. What positive triggers seem to fuel my resilience, and what negative triggers seem to dampen my effectiveness?

2. Eyes, mind and heart wide open

The Oracle's quilt

Soldier A

After the Anzac Day dawn parade on our Special Forces base, everyone gets together to connect over some much-needed coffee. Soldier A has been retired for some time but continues to attend the base's memorial service.

As he approaches the couch in the base's common room, those who are sitting down shuffle to make space for him. His knees and hips have been damaged by decades of carrying heavy packs and parachuting into precarious environments behind enemy lines. Even so, he chooses to stand.

His Anzac coat is heavy, fitting for the crisp morning air, but now he is indoors in the warmth, he hesitates to take it off. His shoulder and elbows have been shattered by bullets, so his movement is very limited. It's not the pain he fears though, it's the fuss.

His body is trained to handle all extremes. He shows no discomfort except when words of entitlement or judgement of others are uttered.

For all that he has done, he cringes at the thought of any recognition for himself. His belief in the Anzacs' capacity to do good is so unwavering that he feels privileged to have been a guardian of their legacy.

Despite his humility, he is seen as something of a legend on the base. Legends of his magnitude are often crowded by enthusiastic fans, but not Soldier A. People approach the space around him slowly and mindfully. His fragile frame oozes mana, depth and warmth. Nothing appears accidental in the space he takes, least of all his words.

Soldier A projects his voice gently, as if he has no expectation that anyone needs to hear what he has to say. Yet, when he speaks, the chatter around him stops, eyes turn towards him, movement ceases and the room goes quiet. Even those who are unaware of this living legend seem to sense that his words deserve the space he chooses to share them in.

He's become a legend not only through his deeds, but also through his – sparsely used – words. His few words hold so much power that A is able to make more space for deep, genuine, open, sincere observations. He has learned the importance of observations through all the times when his life has depended on them.

Soldier A is also known as 'The Oracle' because he always seems to know exactly what goes where in the order of life. Perspective gives you that – and his experiences have given him layer upon layer upon layer of perspective.

Soldier A was a master craftsman of perspectives. Somehow, he had not only survived, healed and grown through his experiences, but he had also carefully woven those perspectives, experiences and reflection into a deeply intricate quilt.

Soldier A's carefully tailored quilt contains enough pieces to captivate anyone. The magic of his quilt is that once you found the piece you related to most, you couldn't help but want to explore other perspectives contained within it, be they adjacent to or opposing your own. There was never a struggle, no forcefulness, no resistance to be found in the unbridling of perspectives, instead there was simply a warm invitation to explore.

Somehow, A knew the order of life and was able to move through its peaks and troughs lightly, making way for good as he went. The story goes that in the jungles of Asia, Soldier A once made peace with a venomous snake that joined him in his primitive shack. His reason for doing so was a pragmatic commitment to avoiding the ferocity of the oversized local rats. The snake would hunt down the rats before they had the chance to obliterate A's meagre provisions.

On another mission, Soldier A nurtured a herb garden in his front yard. Soldier A would have been disappointed if anyone had asked why he'd bothered planting a garden when he could have lost his life at any moment. After all, it wasn't entirely up to him when that might happen, but it was his prerogative to influence his environment and take whatever actions available to him to make improvements and give himself something to look forward to, no matter where he was.

He'd say, 'You can find your capacity for influence even if you are confined in something as tiny as a matchbox. Whether you will see the opportunity is up to you.' This was a pillar of A's resilience. He would find something to improve or influence for the better, no matter his circumstances.

Soldier A's ability to find and build common ground with adversaries was legendary. Among his reported honours were countless missions to rescue innocent civilians across three continents and hostage negotiations at the highest level.

More important for the team though, was his ability to nurture generations of soldiers. One of Soldier A's favourite sayings was: 'The most effective way to make it through the enemy, be that the enemy within or beyond, is not the power of bullets but of understanding.'

This alone seems to take superhuman power. Where does one get the strength to stand with understanding when in volatile conditions?

According to Soldier A, maintaining your equilibrium or being relatively unaffected by what is happening around you is not always a good test for resilience. 'Sometimes being impacted by the events around you springboards you into otherwise inaccessible levels of resilience.' Then he added, 'To heal and grow, first you have to feel.'

Soldier A was weaving a quilt.

It took me years to eventually work out why a quilt that contained some of the most confronting patterns of human behaviour could feel so empowering, so positive, so wonderful to sit with. It was because every one of those patterns was wrapped in learning, growth and gifting. Soldier A had transformed every one of the challenges he had confronted into something good. In every case, he had improved, whether by learning from loses or pain, or by creating better outcomes through his influence.

He had woven lives across corners, building connections and pathways to healing and gratitude. He would never speak of himself or those around him as victims of events. He'd only speak of predicaments in a way that showed others the path to growth and healing.

If someone was to make a statue symbolising resilience it would look like Soldier A. How could someone who had witnessed some of the darkest nuances of humanity be so open, generous and warm? It was as if A had an endless well of resilience. In fact, the more demanding the challenges, the fuller his resilience well had become. What was his secret?

He told me, 'Reacting to what you think is happening or how you think things need to be – that's not resilience. You have to pay utmost respect to every situation you create or encounter. You need to give it your attention and craft your engagement carefully. Every situation deserves your best. That's how you craft resilience.'

Because of that belief, A had left every situation he encountered better than he found it. His resilience criteria was: 'Never giving in on making better; always looking out to improve someone's lot. After a while, you stop seeing things as good or bad. Every situation carries learnings and opportunities to do something good.'

Soldier A would argue that resilience, like happiness, is not something you go about pursuing. Resilience, like happiness, is a gift you get when you realise you have given a situation your best and your all. He'd advise that 'to change your relationship with any tricky nuances of your life, you have to add learning'.

Tough people come from tough places

We often confuse resilience with toughness. This is probably because resilience has historically been studied selectively through the stories of people with superhuman grit, who have endured almost incomprehensible levels of strain, stress and challenge.

Tough people *do* come from tough places, but toughness is not the object of resilience. Indeed, toughness often gets in the way of resilience, leading instead to fixedness and rigidity, leaving us blind to the uniquely nuanced lessons that every exposure promises to deliver. Meanwhile, tough places have as many unique nuances and details as there are people. You have probably been to a tough place or two and made it through. The question is: how well? Did you arrive at the other side a better person than you were before?

Many of the 'heroes of resilience' in the SAS, for example, shared that their journey to service and their toughest experiences in service were nothing compared to what they had come from. While some of us crumble in the face of trials, many people who confront hardship learn to anticipate it. They develop strategies to deal with crisis, change and ambiguity in whatever form it takes.

SAS operators are selected and trained for hardship, so that – with every challenge they survive – their scripts widen and deepen and their confidence develops. After a while, what once seemed overwhelming for them becomes just the stuff of life. In the words of one SAS trooper: 'You think you have arrived at the resilience panacea when you realise that all situations, however novel they may seem, are a little like something else you have experienced in the past. You therefore anticipate what's ahead and handle it.' Clearly, that was not entirely true.

We have all developed readiness based on past experiences. However, as one of the entrepreneurs I work with would say, 'Sometimes your experiences are your greatest asset, but sometimes they can be your biggest hinderance.'

The challenge is to remain open to possibilities.

Tool: Nurturing my resilience

Reflect on the question: did you arrive at the other side a better person than you were before?

Look back and look ahead.

Look back through some of the challenges you have overcome or the ones you are still working through. Consider what you have gained, hope to gain or may gain from navigating these challenges resiliently.

Draw a tree. At the *roots* of each tree, list each challenge – current or past – in turn. Consider that the source of your growth, be that growth and learning from challenges you have overcome or from those you may commit to pursuing.

At the *trunk* of each tree, list the support or strategies you have employed in the past or hope to have in order to grow or learn from this challenge.

At the *top* of the tree, list the learnings or gains you have made from the challenges you have overcome, and the ones you hope to gain in the future.

Reaching out for vulnerability

The most resilient amongst us consider their resilience to be a well-practised muscle. Their resilience instincts flex and shred to fit the specific test of their circumstances, allowing them to surpass, dominate and overcome the obstacle until … 'Until' is a pivotal word for those who demonstrate the kind of ever-evolving, adaptive and enduring resilience we all seek.

For them, resilience was not the answer to the question, 'How will you handle it?' Handling 'it' had become a given by virtue of being alive. Their questions with regard to resilience were along the lines of: 'Did you grow through it? How quickly? How will you serve through your learnings?'

The most resilient people I worked with all knew that being tough was a short-term survival strategy, an overplayed innate instinct. Confronting as it was for them, they'd realised that, when you take the shine away, toughness is just the same as fragility – a coping mechanism on the other side of the same continuum of replayed scripts. If you overplay it or stay with toughness for too long, you'll inevitably slide to the other side of the continuum – to fragility.

When it comes to resilience indicators, our personalities and the range of our habitual responses can often be reduced to learned patterns in the form of a rendition of the fight/flight/freeze response.

- I fight – I am tough.
- I flee – I avoid for fear of being fragile.
- I freeze or disengage – I hope the storms will blow away above my head.

Resilience is learning when to let go of being tough and reaching out towards vulnerability.

This can only be done when you can recognise your triggers, and when you know your own vulnerabilities and those of the people around you.

The resilience heroes I studied thought that the capacity to 'survive, surpass, dominate and overcome' was all they needed for resilience. Until they realised that they were repeating the same script and missing the nuances of the new. The new, however confronting at first, always contains a springboard to the next iteration of resilience they were seeking. Instead of diving into it with bright eyes and bushy tails as demanded by resilience, their readiness – developed through the hardships they had tackled in the past – meant that they had learned to pre-empt novel situations to the detriment of the unique. In the words of one SAS member: 'My pivot to greater resilience was in noticing the difference between awareness, alertness and assumption.'

Awareness demands openness, honesty and vulnerability.

Alertness offers readiness, but also limits perceptions to what has been, rather than what could be. If resilience is all about being better than when your predicament found you, then running on alertness is simply not a good enough tool for resilience. In fact, in the complex environment we all operate in, alertness is nothing more than an exaggerated stress response. It has a nostalgic appeal at best, but it also has poor functionality.

Alertness attunes our senses to match our expectations, decreasing the importance of everything that doesn't fit. It is designed to deploy the equivalent of your attention's SWAT team to protect you from a purported perpetrator a week after they have been arrested.

Interpersonal conflict or tension is something many of us have experienced. In this context, alertness is like walking back into the same office a year after you changed jobs because of a particularly difficult colleague, who has since also left. While you are alert to the culture of the place, you may fail to notice that everyone had your back all along and they're excited to see you. Worse, you might even act in a defensive manner even though none of your ex-colleagues were responsible for how you were treated.

Assumptions? They're the lazy way out. They offer a script for the mind in the absence of solid proof. When we run on assumptions, we constrict our entire world to the limited scope that overused biases can offer. Some of the assumptions we draw can be helpful. At the very least, they reduce the cognitive burden of us needing to pay attention to new situations in their entirety. They offer respite by giving us shortcuts to the conclusions we draw about people and situations.

Just as often, assumptions can be harmful or at least, limiting. They reduce our scope for exploring the unique and the new, for connecting and for learning. We have all felt the discomfort of wrong assumptions that others may have drawn about us. They sit as oddly as a poorly fitting sweater borrowed at an unplanned sleepover. Unchecked, assumptions can stick. A day in that sweater might be OK, but any longer will likely reduce you to a disgruntled visitor in your own life.

So, will you commit to standing where your feet are, eyes, mind and heart wide open? Pause and reflect for a moment on what depletes you. As you are holding that thought in your mind, can you see the line between alertness, awareness and assumptions?

How can you make space for greater awareness, minimise the emotional and cognitive demands of your alertness and reduce the blinker effect of assumptions?

To reduce assumptions, invite or consider different views or ways to interpret events.

To reduce the impact of alertness, broaden your readiness stance.

|

Fuelling your resilience engine

Change, stress and ambiguity will always find us, and – whether we like it or not – they will unwrap some of the narratives we've attached to our identity.

If we are lucky, the changes we experience will have strengthened us enough to trust that we can stand confidently in our own story and intentions, benevolently oriented to the world. But, if you've been running around depleted without having refuelled, the next unexpected detour on your journey of life will see you stall. Your resilience engine does not care whether your next detour is straight or windy. It only cares about the amount of fuel it needs to keep going. This is true for all of us.

Imagine you're driving a car, which has an empty fuel tank, in peak-hour traffic and you're running late for the most important meeting of your career.

Are you anxious?

How do you react to the overly cautious driver blocking your way from changing lanes to the exit you have to take?

Your focus is laser sharp on all the things that could go wrong. It's almost as if you think that if you can just stay focused and minimise disruptions, the fumes in your fuel tank will get you to your meeting on time.

Just as your car has a fuel tank, so your body has a resilience tank. Some of us are better able to tell when our tank is getting low and act pre-emptively. Some only notice the flashing 'empty tank' light when it is too late to take the exit off the highway and refuel. In most cases, setbacks, unexpected jolts and challenges tend to find us unprepared.

Resilience is seldom tested in the predictable or the known. Even so, there are gains to be made if you are in this tricky place.

- Learn how to manage your resources effectively in the future and be pre-emptive.
- Realise that stressing about running on empty will not refuel your tank. Instead, pause and consciously choose how you will use the little you have left to make it through.
- Recognise that what you may see as triggering when running on empty is seldom worth your reaction.

The stress of running on empty to get to your destination does not have to affect your experience of being there. These are distinct events. Managing yourself in the moment as well as in transitioning from one event to the next, without spilling over negative load, is key.

Many of us get to know the subsets of that vital self-awareness by making it through some of the darkest episodes of our lives. We learn our triggers by being triggered. We learn the scope and span of our innate strength through our biggest trials. We define our most treasured things by the critical moments of our lives.

There is some merit to doing these things, but resilience in retrospect is only useful in research. In our daily lives, the resilience that matters is that which we demonstrate in our present challenges and in how we manage our baseline so the next challenge can see us at our best. Resilience is seldom meaningfully measured in reactions. It is, however, always found in the deliberate choices we make. Soon, we will explore strategies for maintaining and building our baseline, but for now, the challenge for us is to maintain awareness in the moment.

Tool: My resilience bucket

Someone once said that resilience is like a bucket. We can fill our bucket with things that support our resilience. These may include the people we love, experiences we treasure, and rituals, habits and routines that make us feel grounded and strong.

There are also things that drain our bucket. For some, this might include conflict at work or work pressures, family pressures, health concerns or global issues.

The proposition is simple. At the very least, to maintain or strengthen our resilience, we need to keep a balance between what fuels us and what drains us. Better than that, we can change our perspective and prioritise in order to minimise what depletes us and maximise what fuels us. Let's try this:

1. Above the bucket pictured over the page, write down examples of things that fill your resilience bucket, that fuel you and give you strength.

2. Below the bucket, write down the things that drain your resilience bucket.

3. Now shift your attention to the circle of control. Under the heading 'Control', write a list of the things that deplete you that are within your control.

4. Under the heading 'Influence', write a list of the things that aren't within your control but that you can have some influence over.

5. Under the heading 'Indulgence', write a list of the things you cannot do anything about.

6. Reflect on how you might improve your resilience by focusing your energy on the things you can influence or control. How might you adapt your approach so that you can gain control over what may seem uncontrollable?

7. Reflect on the things that fill your bucket. How might you invest more of your time, focus and energy on making these more accessible for yourself?

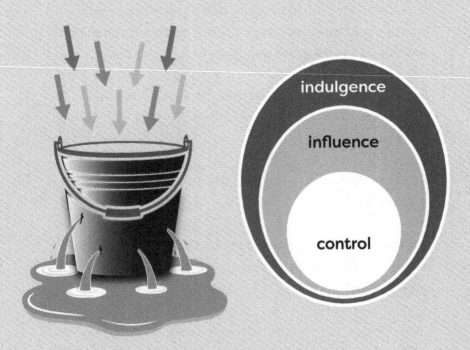

Three key reflection points

1. We don't need breakdowns to have breakthroughs. At the very least, we don't need the same crises or breakdowns played on repeat. What makes some of the most remarkable humans worthy of learning from is that they are able to recognise critical junction points and to pivot away from a potential crisis – be that within themselves or in their external environment – before it turns into a disaster or a breakdown.

2. We can gain resilience by disrupting the flow of the habitual stresses we sometimes indulge in. This also applies to disrupting the tendency to carry negative load from one distinct situation to the next. Often, we are the only thing in common between distinct moments in our lives and we have the freedom to choose how to show up.

3. Resilience is often the by-product of a string of small wins; tiny, deliberate changes that collectively create tectonic power shifts. Most of us are wired to do the heroic when a real crisis hits. However, the stresses that deplete our resilience daily are seldom about true crisis and are more often about the tiny piece of grit in our shoe. At first, this stressor can be an irritant you notice but can move ahead with. No matter how tiny it is at first, you cannot run a marathon with it there without feeling pain. Unless you pause and shake that grit out of your shoe, it will eat away at your resilience.

In most cases, shifting an event or a trigger from all-too-familiar negative stress to a positive opportunity is simply a matter of conscious relabelling or reframing.

Let's pause here for a minute. Are we speaking of the same self-awareness that most of us walk around with? For many of us, it seems, self-awareness is the exact thing that distracts us from our goal and from our resilience.

We are preoccupied with the reasons why we should be feeling anxious prior to what we perceive to be a significant event. We wear our past hardships like Scouts wear badges on their jerseys. We craft whatever story we tell ourselves about those experiences to remove ourselves from the centre stage of our own lives. We avoid, ruminate, worry, agonise, combat and refrain because we are self-aware, don't we?

I posed that question to one of my interviewees, trying to align my concept of self-awareness with his in order to extract the exact definition he had in his mind, which was so crucial to resilience.

He politely interrupted me as I was rattling off examples of 'self-awareness' misconstrued – the sort of versions of it I see constraining human potential in my practice. With the firm-but-friendly approach you'd expect of someone who has discipline of mind, he said: 'That's not self-awareness, that's self-pity – a debilitating indulgence of the mind.'

And there it is. Self-awareness is knowing where your inclinations come from, but also knowing what to select, interpret and deselect so that your state supports your goal and, even more importantly, allows you the discipline to act in the direction of your desired outcome.

This kind of awareness comes with another form of discipline – that of knowing how much of what comes to our minds to consider and in what way to consider it for your awareness to yield the resilience benefits you seek. In managing the acute, this discipline is underpinned by the knowledge that stress expands with the space you give it.

My interviewee is right. Many of us are indulgent in perpetuating worry way past its point of usefulness. The more we perpetuate this, the less resources we have available to manage demands with and the more porous our resilience becomes. Soon enough, the pebbles in our shoes become boulders that block us.

Tool: Recalibrate in the moment

Self-talk can significantly affect our confidence and resilience. As such, we cannot ignore negative thoughts for too long. We must address them, process them and take the appropriate action to dispel worry and rumination. Here is a simple but powerful exercise to dispel negative self-talk.

1. Draw four columns. In the first column, list some of the negative thoughts that get in your way most often.

2. For each thought, ask yourself, 'Is this a fact?' Write your answers in the second column. If it's not true 100 per cent of the time answer no. If it is true, ask yourself whether you believe it is a helpful or productive thought for you.

3. For each thought, consider what would be a more productive thought to have instead. Write these in the third column, perhaps adding something you would say in the face of a challenge.

4. In the fourth column, list your past successes. For every past success, provide three statements to back it up, things that give you the right to think your positive thought.

Changing your mindset

Those trained to thrive in ambiguity have mastered a mindset that seems enviable at first, but that is easy to develop. This mindset stipulates that change, threat and ambiguity are not only normal but essential to thriving. As one of my interviewees said, 'It's a gift, but not always a well-wrapped one!' Sometimes, in fact, it's not wrapped at all, but it's a gift, nonetheless.

The most resilient among us orient themselves towards shifts and changes with anticipation, openness, grace and even gratitude. They relish the possibility that they are about to grow some more. They approach positive outcomes, such as success and validation, with the same attitude as failure and criticism. They call this resilient neutrality, and it is their fuel for thriving in ambiguity. But let's not confuse this with ambivalence. Resilient neutrality is active and restless – an intent in action. It is the utmost appreciation of the importance of the subtle nuances in the stance we need to take when we (willingly or otherwise) step into the unknown.

Every shift in our context, especially the unforeseen and the unprecedented, should be engaged with respectfully, with our hearts, minds, eyes and arms wide open. Through this mindset, doubt, fear and anxiety transform into purposeful action.

This will fuel your confidence that 'being better always' is not only essential but also attainable. Such is that confidence in those well-versed in resilience, one of them even said:

The unknown is what excites me. I seek out uncertainty for therein is my challenge and my chance for growth.

Pivot towards your best

Assumptions and alertness are quick switches designed to help us minimise the anticipated cognitive and emotional burdens of new encounters. They base themselves on top of existing patterns we have formed or gathered over time. Rather than perceiving the whole picture in its novel nuances, patterns invite a quick search for fit.

Our brains are designed to draw and collect predictions that are based on current or common perceptions of our experiences. They are neatly folded layers of things we hear, see or believe we have experienced and therefore we anticipate we may experience again.

Self-preservation means that even the optimists among us register risks and the potential for failure more easily than the possibility for success when tackling the unknown. The only difference for the more resilient among us is that they are more ready to tackle whatever is ahead and they set their expectations to the best outcomes, not the worst. It is not prepare for the worst, hope for the best. It is consider the worst, work to the best.

When tested, fearful or depleted, we tend to anticipate outcomes in a way that will minimise harm to us or prepare us to protect ourselves from harm. The exact approaches we take may differ depending on our personality, values and past experiences.

When this is done in haste, we typically opt for the familiar rather than the optimal. We are wired to reduce uncertainty and the chaotic mix of emotions that uncertainty inevitably produces.

Resilience lies in the tension between the experiences we are grounded in and the greatest possibilities our creativity, will and vision for ourselves can generate. Resilience is all about maintaining balance on the spinning edge of possibilities.

Triggers

Triggers can be found no matter your circumstances. They travel along with you however much you think you are hiding. They are within you and not in your context. Knowing them is not enough for self-awareness and, therefore, for resilience. Knowing what you come with is not enough. You need to know what to rest on, what to watch out for and what to let go of when your mettle is tested. You have to act in a way that minimises the risk of them perpetuating their place in your life.

The fluctuating concept of self

I came across someone who said, 'To know yourself is to accept you don't'. This stuck with me, inviting reflections and discussions with colleagues. We should all embrace this if we are to embark on building true resilience. I choose this to mean that we simply do not realise how much we can amaze ourselves if we only let ourselves be intentional in the way we engage with every moment. After all, resilience demands constant evolution.

You lose self-awareness the minute you stop developing it. Resilience and self-awareness require the same attention as crossing a busy highway. The minute you stop paying attention, you run the risk of being run over by the traffic of distractions and irrelevant thoughts.

The things we think or say about ourselves are seldom the complete truth, for no other reason than that not even we are aware of the full picture in its detail. Who we are is often a twice or even a thrice-reflected image of us.

This fluctuating concept of self is often within us, even if we can easily default to blaming the world around us. Past trauma, the words someone once uttered to us that have embedded themselves into our conscious mind – we choose to engrave those experiences by constantly repeating the negative narrative we have selected for ourselves at one point in time. We use it as negative reassurance for ourselves. It is a safer way to be, it seems.

This works a little like the grooves being cut into a piece of melted vinyl, ready to be played on the turntable of our lives on repeat. Remember, you can always change the soundtrack to your life.

Tool: Complete the sentence

Sometimes the difference between us strengthening and depleting our resilience can lie in one small word – 'yet'.

We can remain stuck in negative experiences or memories that become fixed narratives for our lives, limiting our opportunities ahead. We can be slower to recognise that, no matter the experience, there is always something we can do about our predicament; there is always space for growth and perseverance. Here are some examples of this:

I was treated badly therefore I am hesitant to engage.
versus
I was treated badly therefore I am hesitant to engage,
yet I maintain hope that most people are well-intentioned
and I strive to broaden my social circles.

I failed as a kid so I fear committing to my dreams again.
versus
I failed as a kid so I fear committing to my dreams again,
yet I continue to try.

Adding a comma and a new phrase after the negative narrative we have formed for ourselves makes all the difference. I was/did/felt, yet I ...

Consider some of the negative or depleting statements you currently attribute to yourself and your life. How might you reframe these in order to open space for greater resilience ahead by adding 'yet'?

Twisted mirrors

Have you ever been in one of those mirror mazes at the circus? All it takes is concave or convex of an unexpensive mirror to give us a distorted view of reality. Stare at that exposure long enough and it will fuel your perception of what you think others think of you. Rather than deciding who you are for yourself, you think, 'I am who I think you think I am.'

The view we adopt of ourselves profoundly shapes our lives. It determines what we assess is possible and attainable for us. Our context, what we select from it and how we select to engage with it can filter out or amplify different nuances of ourselves, shining a light on fragments of our potential as well as our vulnerabilities.

Self-awareness goes far beyond a rather fixed set of readily available descriptors. Especially at the levels required by resilience, self-awareness demands more of a true litmus test on the 'now'. It requires knowledge of *how we are and why we are* the way we are right now. Answering these questions about ourselves requires strength and continuous self-discovery.

Resilience demands that we have the courage to pause and be open to understanding whatever version of us knocks on the door in that moment, whether it be a blustery night or a blissful Sunday. It lies in the knowledge that we are capable of far more than is allowed by any of the limited reflections of ourselves we have been entertained by thus far.

On the journey to thriving no steps can be skipped and no shortcuts can be taken. The first step requires the deepest, most expert knowledge of who it is that is standing here ready to meet the opportunities that are on their way.

You are the expert on you! How you see yourself can depend on whether you will choose a mirror to amuse yourself with or whether you will look in and define yourself by your own vision of your potential.

Experience invariably shows that those who naively take on the journey to thriving in the absence of self-awareness will give in or sidestep along the way, often citing an unbearable burden of self-doubt. Put simply, lack of self-awareness is not only about whether you will make it or not, but it is also about where you are heading, why and with what.

Regardless of the chaos unfolding around us, or the factors throwing us off balance, to engage effectively we need to be firmly aware of the resources we have at our disposal, what we need in order to unlock them and exactly which ones we need to utilise in our current situation. This can mean physical resources, but it always involves intrinsic ones – our own authentic and accessible 'wealth'.

If we have mastered self-awareness, then what this first step demands is checking in with self.

- How did this event shift find me?
- What are the vulnerabilities it's made evident?
- What strengths has it illuminated as essential for me to move forward with?
- What have I learned from this exposure?
- How will I integrate this event to see me thrive?

If we are paying attention to the importance of this exercise of life, we have to do a little better than answering a short list of questions every now and then.

3. Mind where your mind goes – mindful attention

It's a wet Wednesday morning. The sun hasn't risen and the shortest day is yet to arrive. How much shorter of a day can I handle with my ever-diminishing energy? This is a year I want to pass quickly. My heart skips a beat. Am I wishing my days away? I jump in my car to go to a place I dread. I could take this drive to work blindfolded. Today could be a Monday or a Friday but because it's Wednesday the challenge of being stuck in this dull déjà vu sucks a little more. Why am I repeating the same stuff I dread reliving yet again? What am I choosing and what am I omitting to choose?

I have become a passive observer of my own life. It's as if someone is forcing me to watch a movie that promises nothing more than a few lost hours. I am in a fog of chronic burnout. No matter how big or small it is, the next challenge will stop me like a deer in headlights. For the longest time my foot has been on the accelerator, but my engine has been in neutral.

What will it take for me to change this? I don't have the energy to find the energy to get myself out of this cycle.

My Monday mornings have been infused with anxiety for months. It's the kind of anxiety that is quiet enough to be masked by superficial interactions but spiky enough to cause consistent discomfort. I hear this white noise of misguided worry ringing in my ears the minute I mute the distractions. All I want is for my head to be back on my pillow again, but when it eventually gets there, I know my brain will race, preventing my body from shutting down.

I move through molasses all week to get to the two days that have somehow been designated for being happy. I spend the weekend trying to wash away the dullness of the preceding five days just in time to go back to work again.

There is no real reason for this angst. I'm in my first big corporate role out of uniform and I am a grown-up parent. I know that the way I perceive my external world does not occur in a vacuum but rather within the rich context of my internal world. I know that feeling depleted and unhappy makes me more likely to find reasons to justify how I feel. I also know it will take conscious effort for me to find reasons to feel differently.

As I hear myself whinge, I try the 'meanwhile' strategy. It goes like this:

'You are so entitled! You're moaning about your weekend, *meanwhile* Naraya is dreaming about one day being allowed to drive a car. *Meanwhile,* Aisha is hoping her 12-year-old daughter can go to school someday. *Meanwhile,* Anna is praying for something more than a life spent sifting through the rubbish dumps of Sofia. *Meanwhile,* Zaida is hoping her malnourished son will make it through until morning.'

Meanwhile makes things worse! It makes me feel like I should be doing something else entirely with my time. The guilt and sadness amplify. There are so many important things for me to focus on. Instead, I am majoring in minor parts of life.

I try to distract myself with some basic appreciation and gratitude. I think of the privilege of having a job that allows me flexibility. I am grateful for my health insurance and my decent paycheque. Still, I feel as misaligned to my values as possible.

I wonder whether others in the office are playing a similar game. They start each day trying to look good, smell good, smile, so that we collectively feel like we're doing something worthwhile. But this is at once the pain of this moment and the gift of it. I feel loved by all my colleagues, loved enough to know they too feel misaligned. They too feel they must keep going. The more of us who stay in the game, the more of us feel we must continue to choose the game.

My assignments seem pointless. I know I could create remarkable, felt, sensed, tangible, healing shifts for people in our neighbouring community, if I was allowed to invest one-tenth of the amount of resource and energy that goes into my current assignment. Is there a point at which this game stops being justified, and I'll feel free to be honest? What am I missing here?

At home at the end of the day, instead of being present with my child I'll be thinking of the work I need to do. Later, I'll rush through mandatory small talk with my stressed-out husband, so that I can gain the freedom to jump back into a pointless PowerPoint presentation. My negative mindset is in overdrive. I have stripped any semblance of meaning out of my day.

My mind goes back to the handful of merciless critics I've encountered in my life and their words feel *big, loud* and *true* despite the fact so many others have shown me I am worthy. I open a drawer in my mind that is neatly packed with painful memories of heartbreak, frustration and disappointment. I replay past conflicts in my mind.

Suddenly, I realise that my mind has not been where my feet are the whole day, the whole month even. Instead, I've been in pre-play or replay mode and I have set the search engine of my mind to fit the idea of a wet Wednesday at its worse.

I realise that none of the people I've thought about and ruminated over have thought about me for anywhere near the length of time that I've thought about them. I recall the words of David Foster Wallace:

You'll stop worrying what others think about you when you realise how seldom they do.

I have put critical voices of the past on at full blast inside my head. I have been grinding down deep grooves into my mental record in order to produce the sounds I dread the most. The more I replay the dull and frustrating, the deeper the grooves get and the more I believe that this is my lot. I have wedged those sad narratives for life deep into the vinyl of my soundtrack for life. I am wedging my existential nightmares into my day. I am choosing to play the soundtrack of a hum-drum life.

Instead of listening to the noise in my head, I play my favourite The Prodigy track, 'Mindfields'. My rage turns into a smile.

I am completely aware that I have control over my emotions. I choose them, I generate them. I am the one that writes the narrative for my life. I have control over my thinking and, even though I don't yet know the exact actions that will spur me ahead, I know I need to choose the thoughts and emotions that will drive me there.

I start to feel self-compassion. I'll admit, I used to find this term cringeworthy as it is something I wasn't brought up with. In my world, self-compassion seemed indulgent, selfish, a premise occupied by the weak. The truth is, though, that if I took a minute to be kinder to myself, I could do so much good and source so much more strength to help others.

Some years ago, my coach at Christchurch's Institute of Counselling walked me through a series of deceptively simple questions. I found them frustrating. I couldn't tell whether they were backed up by research or theory. She stuck with them, calmly smiling in the face of my sarcasm, inviting me to move past my hard front and work with my heart. She knew that this hardness was a mask, a roaring beast of hurt, a blanket preventing my lack of trust from crippling me. Then she said:

Sit yourself on your knee, and look at all the good that you have done, all that you have achieved. Think of the values you have chosen to nurture in your life. Tell yourself 'No matter what you do, I love you anyway. No matter what you do, I love you anyway.'

Despite my misgivings, I sat myself on my knee and uttered the words I wished I'd had wedged into the grooves of the record of my life – words of love, of being worthy.

She'd say, 'You don't use self-compassion to feel better. You use it because you recognise that you feel bad.'

The next step my coach wanted me to take – fierce self-compassion – was a step too far for me at the time. However, her guidance around it made a lot of sense. It included:

- recognising and identifying my own needs and values
- recognising that my pain is not unique

- opening up to others and seeking support
- providing for my needs first
- motivating myself towards what I needed
- defending my own emotional space by choosing to observe rather than absorb unkindness from others.

The list went on, but my journey to self-compassion was even longer.

Treat yourself like you are someone you are responsible for helping.

These are the words of Jordan Peterson, one of the most famous psychologists of our time. Irrespective of what you might think about Jordan's wider teaching, this rule is impactful and it could make a world of difference to your resilience, too.

Tool: Sit yourself on your knee

When you are depleted or you're managing the onslaught of multiple demands for extended periods of time, you can become overwhelmed and lose hope in your ability to persevere.

When you're feeling this way, sit yourself on your own knee! Show yourself compassion, care, nurturing and appreciation for yourself exactly as you are today.

We often remember the outcomes of our actions and decisions, but forget how we got there. Walk yourself back to some of the dimly lit alleyways of your memory. Think back to the decisive moments in your life where you have overcome a challenge, pushed past doubts or scooped up the hope it took you to keep going.

This is not about the achievements and accolades through which others may recognise your strength. It is about the decisions you have made and the choices you have committed to, which have led you to what may be visible to others. It is about the things others may not know about you but that define you.

Recall the pivot points or difficult choices you have committed to and the easy options you have forsaken in pursuit of a goal or to make things better.

Think about the times when you thought the challenge was greater than you, but you managed to overcome it.

Scribble down times and events that come to mind and will mean something only to you and maybe those closest to you.

Pull back as many of those memories as possible. Sit in them. Acknowledge your strength, your values and the gifts you have pieced together for yourself. Spend a moment appreciating these.

Find gratitude and appreciation for yourself. However depleted you are today, these gifts are still yours.

Our moods can affect our environment

We know that our environments can affect our moods. Entire industries are based on this premise. But equally important is the fact that our emotions can infuse our external environment with things that mimic and match our internal word. Our inner worlds select things that reflect the predictions we make about what our outer world has in store for us. We like to move in sync with our predictions. A pinch of love makes food taste better because of the serotonin it brings. Equally, if you're in a good mood, your meals will always taste better than when you're not.

The way in which we sense and decode our external world does not occur in a vacuum but rather within a rich context of internal physiological and psychological states.

Whether we feel negatively, neutrally or positively charged in the moment determines the sensory cues we will select from our environment. If we don't put a thought to it, we will look for external cues that synchronise with our negative feelings. Our senses are set to seek guidance from our emotions. Our sensory system is cued and charged and ready to go long before any external stimuli come along.

Once brought into action, the senses mimic and mirror our emotions, so if we feel fear, we'll seek out anything – sights, sounds, smells, tastes – that supports our reasons to be fearful, while being slower to notice anything that will make us feel safe.

This brings to mind the words often accredited to the philosopher Lao Tzu:

Watch your thoughts, they become your words.
Watch your words, they become your actions.
Watch your actions, they become your habits.
Watch your habits, they become your character.
Watch your character, it becomes your destiny.

Our mood can change the way we perceive ourselves in the long term as well as in the moment. If we stay fixed in the negative for too long, one episode of negative mood or thought can turn into negative self-perception.

Rather than staying fixed, consider that moods can pass like the weather. We cannot control them, but we can learn to observe them, knowing that good, bad or otherwise, they will pass.

Mindful attention

An SAS soldier we will call Sam once said to me:

Mind where your mind goes.

When it comes to resilience, the mind where your mind goes heuristic – a rule of thumb or guiding principle – has four key ingredients to it:

- self-awareness
- calm and clarity

- deliberate focus
- adaptive coping.

Though each ingredient is distinct, they all build onto the next to help sustain resilience.

1. Self-awareness

Mind where your mind goes is fundamentally about understanding your emotions and using them as a guide to enable you to better engage with the challenge at hand.

One SAS member defined the self-awareness required for resilience as 'understanding how you respond to different triggers, what thoughts to rely on and watch out for in different situations.' To be resilient, you first need to recognise that you can carry your strengths and vulnerabilities along with you from one situation to the next. Knowing yourself and your derailers means you learn how to mitigate the risk of them affecting you negatively.

Self-awareness underpins the ability of SAS members to maintain focus, no matter the obstacles they encounter. They are then able to evolve and adapt during challenges and trials, moving through each challenge in a better state than when they entered it. Through carefully nurtured self-awareness they are better prepared to focus on what matters and discard the white noise that may otherwise occupy their attention.

The white noise creeps in with merciless fury if the SAS members leave the scope of their attention porous. They need focused attention centred on their intent and on the threats and opportunities in their current moment. Porous attention is dangerous and undisciplined. It can lead to countless distractions by absorbing irrelevant input in the present moment or allowing thoughts about the past or future creep into a space that should only be used for pertinent information. No one is immune to the white noise, but some have developed the discipline and commitment to keep it at bay.

2. Calm and clarity

We will explore how to maintain calm and build and sustain clarity in subsequent chapters of this book. For now, I would like to invite you to consider the concept of the panopticon.

The panopticon was invented during the eighteenth century. It allowed the inhabitants of any public institution, including prisons, schools and hospitals, to be watched over by a single guard. The word 'panopticon' has since come to be associated largely with prisons.

Key to its success was that the inhabitants never knew when they were actually being observed. This led them to regulate their own behaviour and act as if they were being watched at all times. For this process to work, the buildings in which the inhabitants were housed were built in a circle with the central point housing the guards.

Panopticons soon lost favour as some of their inhabitants were driven mad by feeling as if they were constantly being watched.

The concept, however, remains useful in that we all volunteer to put ourselves into a form of panopticon. We carry other people's judgements of us as indicative of our potential instead of trusting our self-assessment and any honest, positive feedback we have earned. Instead of embracing opportunities to surpass our limitations, we remain firmly attached to the struggles of our past in hope that alertness will prevent future pain. Looking at other people's life stories on social media, we compare and critique ourselves deeply, not realising that our emotions have reckless disregard for physical distance and time. We let our worth be subject to the number of likes we get on things we post online, as if that will somehow allow us access to happiness. We take the risk of our lives passing us by, choosing instead to fixate on fleeting episodes of past losses and failures or anticipated difficulties.

To be resilient, we have to preserve and protect our strength, our potential and our intimate knowledge of the most authentic version of ourselves. We need to jealously guard our time for reflection and keep building on reasons to be our own most ardent advocate.

3. Deliberate focus

'Build your mindset to pursue what you aim for, rather than what you hope to avoid.' This is the advice you would get from any of the resilience heroes I have studied.

We don't see life as it is, we see life as it can be. That word 'can' opens up an entire world of possibilities if we set our minds to hope, to the possibilities and our intentions. However, it can also leave us depleted and paralyse us if we fail to resolve fear, doubt and negativity.

We try to prove ourselves to others, not realising that it is ourselves that we need to prove something to. What we seem to forget is: 'Wherever we are, there we are!' Unless we change our thoughts, feelings and actions, we will keep seeing the same results.

Changing your external environment won't change your internal thoughts and feelings for long. To change the internal, you have to commit to small deliberate shifts towards improvement, consistently. This can be scary. It can feel like what we crave and desire is beyond our capability. This, we calculate based on what we have felt, known and observed in our pasts. And yet, every new experience allows us to innovate and reinvent.

In most cases, goals we think are way beyond our capacity call for extreme innovation. This frightens us! We wonder, 'Why can't I be fitter/kinder/more determined/braver?' Then, in the gap between what we perceive to be optimal and what we know to be habitual, we freeze.

We cease to realise that the habitual, the suboptimal and the avoidable serve us too. They offset something else entirely. They keep fear of the new at bay. They buffer the effects of doubt, albeit temporarily. They extend the lifespan of comfort at the expense of improvement. When you know, see and recognise this, you can choose to stay where you are or you can choose to *grow* away from it. The way to resilience is through focusing on your intent and committing to daily actions towards your intent.

We are capable of building the most remarkable visions for ourselves. Yet, the words of the Harvard psychologist, William James may ring true for many of us, at least at some stages of our life's. He once said:

> Human beings usually live far within their limits; possess powers of various sorts which they habitually fail to use. They energise below their maximum, and they behave below their optimum.

Avoid the scatter

To build and sustain our resilience, we need to remain focused on what matters. Resilience requires removing the distractions.

Our scattered minds and dislocated attention deplete us, leaving us feeling like life is out of control. Maintaining focus, irrespective of our lifestyle and personal preferences, can be an uphill battle for many of us. We live in environments designed for attention-mining. We find ourselves racing, rushing, barely keeping up with our hyperstimulated brains. There are many simple solutions to this, including basic mindfulness and micro-break practices. We will explore these strategies in later chapters. For now the most important practice is that of reducing the scatter of our attention.

Distractions are cumulative, incessant and sneaky. Distractions are to the mind what fast food or drugs are to the body. The more you have them the more you crave them.

We are all vulnerable to distractions. It is just that some of us, chiefly those who have volunteered to train themselves for the acute, have tangible reminders of the power of focus and experientially inbuilt appreciation for the cost of distraction.

Mind where your mind goes emphasises 'the importance of committing to the desired outcome, to the exclusion of thoughts that may be irrelevant or detrimental to that outcome.' If you commit to choosing and maintaining awareness of where your focus lands in demanding times and deliberately direct your thoughts and attention towards your desired outcome, you are much more likely to achieve your goals.

Another interviewee commented:

Resilience is all about your ability to maintain a disciplined mind, focus on what matters and maintain a connection to what fuels you, rather than what depletes you in every moment.

Mind where your mind goes reminds us to deliberately manage and direct our thoughts and emotions towards positive outcomes and maintain focus and clarity of thought in demanding conditions. In the words of another person I interviewed, it recognises that 'resilience is about being aware of what you allow to occupy the contents of your working memory'.

Another SAS member explained, 'You have to mind your thoughts. You are not able to explore alternatives when your mind has gone into fight/flight/freeze mode or when you excessively worry about what is ahead or ruminate on what has been.'

Crucially, in the context of mind where your mind goes, many people I spoke to referred to it as the individual's capacity 'to explore alternatives, even when it may initially seem their fate is sealed.' Maintaining your focus on intended outcomes and possibilities rather than risks, setbacks or limitations is critical.

The capacity to maintain focus on the bigger goal and on opportunities was consistently acknowledged as key to resilience amongst SAS members. In the words of one interviewee, this is 'because the route to your goal is often peppered with setbacks'.

Mind where your mind goes recognises the critical importance of maintaining a clear and unwavering focus on your goal while resisting tunnel vision. In the words of one soldier: 'It's normal for our minds to drift, but success here requires unwavering focus on intent.'

To achieve complex goals or overcome significant obstacles, you need to learn to exclude factors that are irrelevant or detrimental to your mission from your thinking. You need to think broadly, while being unwaveringly focused on your mission's success.

Maintain your resources

Self-awareness allows us to recognise when our resources are becoming depleted and to seek opportunities to replenish them. In the words of one SAS interviewee, 'When you know yourself, you pay really close attention to what is left in your tank. You can't survive for long on empty.'

Here, mind where your mind goes also highlights a commitment to the unique anchors SAS members rely on to maintain their equilibrium and on the importance of staying mindful and connected.

Resilience demands not only focus on intent but also focus on the source of authentic wealth to carry us to that intent. One interviewee commented: 'You can sometimes lose yourself in the intensity of your challenge; you can lose perspective, become completely engulfed in it. This might help in the short run, but after a while you stop being useful to yourself or others. Your stressed out mind may make you think you are too busy. It wants to keep you on alert. But you need to outsmart the voice of fear. You must steal time to focus on what grounds you, what fuels you.'

Centre on hope and possibilities

Interviewees emphasised that focus on present possibilities and on the positives (rather than ruminating or worrying), be it in the pursuit of short- or long-term goals, is key to maintaining resilience. One SAS soldier I spoke with shared:

I spent eight months preparing [for the selection course] by myself – every hour of every day, without any certainty or support. To get there, I had to clear the decks of sabotaging thoughts daily.

Unless you have the discipline to infuse hope and optimism in tackling the challenge, your perseverance might give in along the way.

The resilience heroes I worked with would argue that 'the most significant challenges are often those that demand physical, emotional and spiritual endurance but offer little respite'. As a part of the mind where your mind goes heuristic, to sustain your resilience, it is crucial that you learn to break things down, acknowledge the wins – however small they may be – and fuel optimism and hope through the feedback of experience.

To support resilience, your focus needs to fuel your confidence, guiding you to take one step at a time. In the words of one SAS soldier: 'When you are confronted with significant challenges, you can sometimes forget that you need to keep your mind on the stepping stones in front of you as well as on your ultimate destination. If you do not break things down, you run the risk of becoming overwhelmed, missing an opportunity or failing to navigate each obstacle effectively.'

Every moment we choose to remain in the wrestle with adversity in pursuit of better deserves to be celebrated.

However little or big these openings for hope may be, they build our resilience baseline, often as evidence of the extraordinary capabilities we never thought we had within our reach. As the SAS would say, these condition the 'never give-in' attitude.

4. Adaptive coping

Managing and regulating your emotions in order to sustain resilience is key. Emotional regulation and adaptive coping play a critical role in resilience. Adaptive coping involves the ability to focus on the challenge at hand without reducing or inflating the scope of the challenge. It also involves the ability to regulate your emotions, and select the responses that can best meet the demands of the challenge. To explain the importance of adaptive coping, one of the interviewees shared:

> Knowing where your head is at is a good starting point. However, knowing how to get it to where it needs to be is far more important.

Mind where your mind goes signals the importance of being deliberate and selective towards constructive responses. Your ability to manage your perceptions and responses effectively can mean the difference between success and failure in testing situations. One SAS member commented: 'You get to learn that some of what you feel and think is really just white noise that does not belong in the here and now. It may be a response to past events or pessimistic future-thinking. Some of that may be useful, but most of it can be detrimental. To be resilient, you need to learn how to cut out the white noise – at least long enough to see yourself past the obstacle.'

The ability to manage your perception is key for selecting the most adaptive response. An ability to use stress as a driver rather than derailer can be pivotal for success. In the words of one SAS interviewee: 'Stress and worry can actually feel physically heavy after a while. The more you know yourself, the easier it gets to realise that all situations, however novel they may seem, are a little like something else you have experienced in the past. You learn to rest on what will aid you and silence what distracts you. To get there, you need to manage your emotions and redirect them towards your intent constructively.'

Maintaining a sense of neutrality about failure and other stressors – resilient neutrality – is also key for gaining a mindset of resilience. By maintaining resilient neutrality, you are more likely to engage with difficult or testing things with reason and objectivity rather than reactivity. In choosing where your mind goes, you are able to engage with the learning opportunities failure can offer while remaining committed to working through limitations with an unwavering focus on positive outcomes.

We all experience self-doubt and we are all prone to self-sabotage at times. By minding where your mind goes, you are granting yourself an opportunity to widen the gap between an event we perceive as negative and how we respond to it. In the words of an interviewee: 'We all have gremlins, self-doubt and self-sabotaging tendencies of one kind or another. Knowing how and when these may present means you can choose to have a conversation with your gremlin and disarm doubt, rather than submerging in self-defeating thoughts or tendencies.'

Resilience demands knowing the difference between helpful and unhelpful interpretations of events, as well as the ability to commit to the most helpful response we can use to engage in our predicament.

One SAS interviewee shared his approach to resilience by saying: 'At no point are you promised that you will have it easy. On the contrary, from the first step you take in this place, you realise that this will be challenging each day and in every way – physically, mentally, spiritually – for you and those you love. Thus, you quickly build the habit of being choiceful with what and how you engage your mind and attention.

'You can focus on all the strains and what life demands from you or you can focus on the positive outcome you can create if you take one step forward. You can give yourself an excuse to pull back and take action that's ultimately destructive, or you can choose to stay committed to the bigger picture, your goal and your vision.'

Another SAS member shared: 'Where your mind goes, the rest of you follows! You have to learn to be deliberate and the more you choose well, the more confident you'll get in your ability to adapt your approach towards your mission's success.'

Tool: Gear up

'Gear up' is a simple tool, based on anxiety-management practices, to help you to reframe, ground and focus. As a practice, it allows you to notice the ways you may need to pivot each day to sustain your resilience. No matter where you are, physically or emotionally, it invites you to be in your present moment with curiosity and commitment to better. Its about the now, not yesterday, tomorrow or a year from now. Here are the steps:

Ground yourself in your present moment as you are, not as you think you should be.
Bring your mind to your present (good/bad/otherwise).
Engage in at least four cycles of deliberate deep breathing.
Wherever you are, look around you and focus on one point for a minute.
See if you can spot a leaf, a tree or a cloud outside. Look at that for a moment.
Wiggle your toes.
Wiggle your fingers.
Roll your shoulders back a few times.
Roll your head a few times.
Tilt your head back and smile.

Engage with what matters right now.
This may mean taking a first step – no matter how small – in the direction of your goal, ticking off something on your to-do list or simply making a cup of tea.

The only rule is, whatever it is you engage with, do it deliberately, intentionally and slowly.

Act to remind you that you can effect positive change.
Engage in deliberately creating a positive effect. Take at least one meaningful action to remind you of the effect you can have on your experience of the world in this moment. Look around, look within. What is one thing you can do right now to help you create a positive shift. Here are some suggestions:

- *Next time you go out, smile at as many people as you can.*
- *If you are driving, let someone go ahead of you, smile and graciously wave them in.*
- *Take the time to say hello to the person who welcomes you at the gym or in a shop. Make them feel like they matter the most in that moment.*
- *Find something to compliment a stranger on.*
- *Buy a cup of coffee for the next person in the queue at your favourite cafe.*
- *Send a friend a note of appreciation.*
- *Pick up a piece of rubbish in the street or at the beach.*
- *Look around your community. Where can you see scope for random acts of kindness?*

No matter how you feel, commit to a positive act every day. Never miss a moment during the in-between times. In fact, make these times be your best and study the gains you make by affecting others.

Reflect daily

What actions or experiences have you generated to shift you towards gratitude, strength, compassion and joy?

Collect your lessons learned and note what you may need to integrate in your repertoire for tomorrow.

Unplug

Notice how your actions have shifted you from the spiral. Gain confidence from knowing you have stored new learnings and a new way of influencing your experience. Be ready to repeat these when the trigger presents itself. Remember that it is simply a temporary state.

Press on

Turn the page and commit to what's next!

PART 2
BELONGING

4.
Choose your place, find your stance

Mr S

Mr S grew up in a poor family and his early life was rife with challenges. His family moved around a lot as his parents searched for employment. His multigenerational, multicultural home brought challenges with it. However, S would always smile when he spoke about his upbringing. His family might not have had much, but love was always abundant in their home.

Some of Mr S's fondest memories were when his life seemed to be the hardest. His family moved to America to find work. There, they had to choose whether to pay for food or for electricity. Their home would go dark at sundown, dinners were cooked on a portable gas stove and, on cold nights, everyone slept together in the living room. S and his siblings were bullied at school. There were no family holidays and the children never went to the handful of birthday parties they were invited to because buying presents was an unaffordable luxury.

Despite all this, the love in their home was abundant and the hugs were plenty. Through this, Mr S learned that his worth was not in what he had, but in what he gave or gained from each day.

The discussions around the gas cooker were the best. Mr S's mum had a rule that everyone had to report on three things from their day:

1. One awesome thing they had noticed
2. One challenge they had overcome
3. One new thing they had learned.

Mr S called this the NOL brief – noticed, overcome and learned.

The depth of connection Mr S experienced as a child lasted him his whole life. It also gave him an unwavering sense of self-worth.

One day when he was being bullied at school, Mr S made his bully cry – but not in the way you might expect. S had realised that his bully was probably a very sad child who must have lacked the vital love Mr S so cherished in his own home. Instead of fighting back, Mr S ran towards his tormentor, arms wide open and said, 'I am so sorry you don't have a warm home. You are always welcome to come to our house. You are so, so very sad. Clearly you don't feel loved. We will be open to loving you, too!'

S felt a deep sense of belonging. Initially, he attributed this sense of belonging to the people who had cared for him so well. But after a while, he grew to realise that the values and nurturing he had been given had made him feel so solid on his feet that he felt a sense of belonging no matter where he was or who was around him. When he became a Special Forces operator, this was to become his superpower. He could make any place a home and anyone a family. The most important thing was that he belonged to himself.

The importance of belonging

One of the remarkable SAS soldiers I worked with used to say:

> Belonging is vital for resilience. Belonging is like gravity. Without belonging you drift aimlessly and off course.

What does belonging mean to you? Cast your mind to the last time you felt you belonged. How did you think, feel and act when you felt you belonged? How did you engage with others around you or with your environment when you felt you belonged?

Belonging is a fundamental human need, and it is vital for resilience that this need is met. Our sense of belonging influences our identity, self-worth, sense of safety, capabilities and capacity to deal with change, ambiguity and unpredictability.

When thinking about belonging, we often think of our upbringing, our culture or our family. For resilience, belonging is not necessarily about exploring your background or culture. It invites you to evaluate and strengthen the sense of belonging you have cultivated for yourself, within yourself, through the values, learnings, experiences and vision you have selected to develop in yourself.

Your resilience is not in what you experience but how you make sense of those experiences and grow from them. The ultimate measure of resilience is in the quality of the narrative you choose for the life you belong to.

Having the knowledge and ability to tackle challenges and the unknown is not enough. To launch your most resilient response, you need solid grounding and deep, enabling belonging. As Bill the Oracle said, 'You need to feel you belong where your feet are, no matter where your feet have landed. Belonging must come from within.' Healthy belonging may sometimes take effort but you have to invest in it because it is vital for your resilience.

Tool: The NOL brief

Every night, before bed, think back over your day and take the time to note:

1. One awesome thing you noticed

2. One challenge you overcame

3. One new thing you learned.

Developing resilience

Resilience sits within our choices, no matter how big or small they are. When we think of resilience, we often focus on its outcomes. How we grow through each experience matters more though. Some outcomes we might see as resilient in the moment may simply be reactions that ultimately deplete resilience. Remember, resilience of the kind we need to thrive evolves, changes and expands as we live. What we rest our resilience on and how we display it may change over time.

Resilience can be pre-conditioned to an extent. There are degrees of resilience that are innate in us, but we can also develop it further through our habits. Habits are patterns formed by actions, and they are rooted in the choices we make consciously or otherwise. Our choices motivate actions, and the repetition of these actions can form habits that either fuel or deplete our resilience.

Resilience doesn't exist in isolation. It has deep roots and broad branches that hold us consciously or unconsciously and we grow attached to them. To build, broaden and fortify our resilience, some of these roots need to be nurtured while some of the branches need to be pruned in the right ways at the right time. One of the most crucial sequences of choices we make when it comes to developing resilience is what, where and how we choose to belong.

The warm home theory

We typically think of belonging in reference to a place, a time, a family or a community. The power of belonging and the ways it supports resilience is almost tangibly visible in people. Among many of the people I have worked with over the years, the impact of belonging is noticeable in that they respond differently to stresses.

As I continued to observe this, I developed a commitment to testing what I had labelled the 'warm home' theory. The criteria for my warm home theory does not necessarily require a home abundant in wealth, stability or physical resources, but it does demand love, connection, being seen, being valued and being important to someone significant – being loved not for what you have, but for who you have chosen to be.

Many of the thrivers and survivors I've met didn't grow up with the privilege of a warm home, at least not in the way Mr S experienced it.

Mother Teresa once said: 'The biggest disease today is not leprosy or tuberculosis, but rather the feeling of not belonging.'

There is an epidemic of loneliness in our society, which has come about through loss of community, loss of purpose and loss of connection. For many of us, that loneliness was exacerbated by the impact of Covid, as so many lives were scattered, our identities bruised and transformed into something unrecognisable. Through it, we lost the crutches that we'd created to hold up the identities we'd built.

How do you live a meaningful life when you cannot even step out your front door? Find the purpose that is closest to you, to your heart, so that you can enhance your capacity to influence the outcomes that matter.

Brian

Brian was a senior executive at an organisation on the brink of a major restructure. He had deep expertise in a highly competitive industry that was rapidly shrinking. If he got made redundant and wanted a job at a similar level in his field, he was faced with moving his family across the globe. He didn't want to do this, so the most likely outcome for him was that he would have to survive on his redundancy pay for long enough that he could retrain in a new industry.

In Brian's childhood, the warm home theory of belonging was not evident. Indeed, he came from an intensely volatile, unstable home, which was – in part – why he was resistant to uprooting his own family. Despite this, he appeared remarkably open, warm, curious and grounded. He showed his best, no matter the situation he found himself in.

Brian was an outlier by every measure. He had achieved the soaring heights of success faster than most. While many of his colleagues were admired from a safe distance worthy of their rank and status, Brian was genuinely loved because he was someone who never spared joy or humility. He seemed to thrive by winning hearts and minds even in the conservative and competitive corporate context. His teams had the highest engagement and productivity scores, and low absenteeism. His success was met with admiration as well as scepticism.

Resilience is contagious. When the inevitable redundancies were announced, Brian's upbeat attitude continued uninterrupted. His focus on galvanising, grounding and energising didn't seem to be swayed. Even though many of them were losing their jobs, his team seemed to welcome the change and, with Brian's guidance, they presented the company's board with ideas about how changes could be implemented faster and more sustainably.

Redundancies are a huge source of stress. Looking into Brian's situation from a worst-case scenario perspective, the expected responses are anger, depression and even suicidal ideation. These often arise from feelings of worthlessness and shame, born out of the realisation that the business people had dedicated themselves to no longer needed them. Stuck in a trance of unworthiness, we'd expect people to sway from grief, through anger and blame, to self-criticism and a sense of failure to a fear of loss for all they had envisioned for themselves ahead.

Brian's positivity was clearly impactful, but it was also confusing and unsettling for some. I even wondered if this was a game to him. How had he skipped the steps of the grief curve and gone straight to acceptance and growth?

As I spoke to him one day, Brian suddenly broke his usual sequence of polite responses to predictable questions: 'Have you heard of JK Rowling? She once said, "And so the rock-solid bottom became the foundation on which I built my life."

'I don't fear this loss. I fear losing my purpose. I am not what I earn, what I have or what I do. I am how I chose to engage in every moment. I don't fear or concern myself with what people think or say about me. I invest my energy instead in doing my best. I don't live in them; I live in me.

'I do all I can to understand their worlds, but never to the extent that I lose the keys to mine. This career is just a vehicle and as all vehicles, it is impermanent. But changing this does not change my purpose. I choose where my feet will go and what my heart will feel. I choose the point to rest my gaze on and the next point I see is so exciting!'

I had heard similar words when interviewing an SAS member about how he managed fear of failure. He said, 'Life has a way to stir and question the vision you have created for yourself, the ideas you hold around who you are or what you want to be. You learn quickly; it is not the "what" that matters. It is your "why" that matters. There are many ways of making your why happen if you are clear on it and own it. If you want to do better for your community, you could do so by being a charity worker, a soldier, a nurse or simply a good neighbour. When you know your why you can change your vessel to get there without getting attached to that vessel. That is what resilience is all about.'

Unlike his colleagues, Brian's identity didn't rely on a set of crutches like his salary, his corner office or his status. He had always been aware of his superpower – the ability to connect with others and see obstacles as opportunities to influence better outcomes. The loss of his job and career meant that he was now free to explore where and how he might contribute without the constraints of corporate targets.

Brian was resilient, but what is far more interesting than his resilient responses was where these responses came from. He had developed the discipline to observe the events around him without feeling engulfed in them. His power was in noticing, in knowing that there is a strength and power within him to pivot his experiences and the experiences of those around him for the better.

He defined himself, not by the acts or omissions of others but his own choices. The identity he had formed for himself was not a reaction to his difficult upbringing but a conscious series of choices. Rather than feeling limited or lacking in some way, he gave himself a world of opportunities. He decided to consciously turn his trials into points of strength. He shared with me once: 'I can sit with anyone because of my upbringing. I have no appetite for judgement. My upbringing invited me to learn psychology, compassion, understanding, patience and, most of all, resilience.'

Through our experiences we create stories. We tell ourselves these stories and we tell the world about us through them, but we can sometimes get stuck in those stories.

Brian was just as likely as everyone else to get stuck in his own stories. Yet, at every tricky junction, instead of seeing challenging events as happening to him, he saw them as invitations to grow. His cumulative experiences of growth and learning through trials allowed Brian to develop deep confidence in his ability to traverse the unknown and to deepen his sense of purpose.

We can get stuck in the trance of unworthiness through self-pity, anger, fear or insecurities. Resilience challenges us to change our relationship with our past; to grow from and add to our story in a way that strengthens us for our purpose. Yes, it takes work, but it is the most important work we can do.

Belonging to purpose

Ama Adhe

What, where and how she chose to belong sustained Ama Adhe's resilience and enabled her not only to survive but also to fuel a powerful legacy. Ama was a Tibetan woman who survived 27 years of imprisonment in horrific conditions. She was starved, tortured and prohibited contact with other prisoners. Only four out of the 300 women that were imprisoned along with her survived.

Ama attributed the power of her indomitable spirit to a deep sense of belonging. In her memoir, *Ama Adhe: The Voice That Remembers*, she described how she made quilts from the clothes of dead prisoners – her friends – as holding onto these pieces of cloth gave her a way to keep the connection with them. Her mission was to return home to see her son again. She also wanted to tell her friends of the people she had met; sharing the grace and uniqueness of those who had passed, so they could keep living by inspiring those who remain.

What can we learn from Ama? To treat challenges and testing situations with the utmost respect by committing to give them our all. The most important gains we can make are in learning and fueling purpose from the trials we encounter.

When tested, mantain focus on your purpose, broaden your perspective. You are not what happens to you but what you do with it.

What did you or could you gain from the experiences you have overcome? Can you will yourself to tell the stories of your trials not as a victim but as a learner?

Sense of purpose

The most resilient people have one thing in common – a clear sense of purpose. Your resilience thrives when you allow yourself to belong and accept that you can be a part of your environment and influence it for the better. No matter what crisis, change or demands you face, belonging to your purpose means you can maintain your balance more easily when in the grip of change.

The starting point to bouncing forward is having your feet firmly planted on the ground and your gaze locked in on the intended direction of your travel – your purpose.

Pursuit of purpose was described by all SAS members as the reason why their resilience prevailed and sustained them in overcoming significant challenges and trials. This was also the case for the most successful athletes I have worked with, including Olympians and Paralympians. Without missing a beat, they too would argue that a belonging to a deep sense of purpose was the reason why they were able to achieve the extraordinary and overcome setbacks. One of the Paralympians I worked with once shared with me:

The weather was closing in. I thought, 'I haven't practised for these conditions,' but I know there are a thousand young boys and girls with disabilities who will be watching me perform. If they have even a second of evidence that this is possible for me, who knows what they will see as possible for themselves. All I need is in this moment. I need to succeed for them, even if it is just one of them for that one second.

The All Blacks say they push themselves to their limits and overcome challenges 'for the jersey'. One purpose they all share is to leave the legacy of the team, represented by the jersey, better than they found it.

It is a push-pull thing. Resilience is called upon when you are pushed to shift away from pain and discomfort, or to adapt to a new status quo. To aid your resilience you also need direction; you need to feel the pull of your goals and your purpose.

Before you start to worry that resilience requires you to immediately set a grand, big purpose for your whole life, accept that for the vast majority of us this grand purpose is a work in progress.

While many of the most resilient people I have worked with have well-articulated life purposes and powerful mission statements, resilience does not demand the grand. When we are experiencing the onslaught of demands, change, ambiguity or loss, the purpose that can sustain our resilience might only apply to this day, this hour or this minute.

Purpose can be found in the immediate, in the tiniest crevices of life, in serendipities. It can evolve and shift with us or it can shift us. It does demand that we pay attention, however, and that we engage with the opportunities it offers when purpose presents itself.

Belonging to the moment

My grandmother used to say, 'In crisis, what matters are the neighbours, the plants and the children – in that order.' I'm convinced she used to put the children last for a laugh, but what matters is that she oriented her mind towards the actions she could take in that very minute to ensure she could have influence over the outcome for the things and people that mattered most to her. This is fundamental for resilience conditioning.

We can take actions to influence our experience and to exert control over our own motivations, behaviours and environments. The more often we do this, the more we prove to ourselves that we can have an impact on the outcomes that matter to us.

Many of us give our resilience away by pouring resources in the direction of things we can do nothing about. This is particularly true when we allow our sense of self-worth to hinge on external things like comparing ourselves to others. You aren't defined by what you have or don't have. In resilience terms, you are defined by your capacity to influence yourself and your environment for the better. This starts with selecting your mindset.

When we traverse challenging times, resilience may be in pausing long enough to ask yourself: how do you serve what matters most now? What about now? What about now? What is the one positive change you can make right now that will influence the outcome of your predicament?

What matters most

Resilience is not an innate ability, as much as it is a practised will. It's about recognising what matters, seeing your intent in your mind and willing yourself to stay focused on it.

This reflection was shared with me during a conversation with one of the remarkable Olympians I support. Her personal mission, vision and purpose formed the core of her sense of belonging. She demonstrated these in her every action. She belonged to her mission and vision, and made it her purpose to inspire and galvanise others to achieve all they could envision for themselves. She said, 'Success takes just two things: vision and sweat.'

What matters most, your vision, may not be the same as what matters now. What matters now may be a step towards achieving what matters most. As an example, what mattered most to her was winning a medal at the Olympics, so that she could inspire and liberate the potential in those who may follow in her footsteps. This would demand preparation that would absorb every minute of her day, full-hearted commitment and sacrifices. However, her family support was what got her to this place, and her bond with her grandparents was deep.

During training camp, some weeks prior to the start of her Olympic campaign, she received the news that her grandmother was unwell. She knew breaking away from training camp would slow her progress, but she also knew that what mattered was time with her family. If she had ignored what mattered in the present moment, what mattered most would have suffered too. Guilt and sadness for not visiting her family would have scattered her motivation.

For her, recognising what mattered most then translating it into taking actions towards what mattered in the now had become a discipline for every day, hour and minute. She practised and pursued this as an athlete and a person. Her recipe for resilience was simple:

- decide what matters most to you
- decide what matters *now* in your pursuit of what matters *most*
- commit and will yourself to stay on it.

Her ability to maintain focus on what matters now, with clear sight on what mattered most, was instrumental in her success. Fuelled by the inspiration she gained from her grandmother, she earned an Olympic medal.

In my case, what matters most is seeing my son happy and fulfilled in exploring the opportunities his world has on offer, developing his passions and his talents, and feeling loved and secure. What matters now for me may be focusing on a work assignment that will help provide broader opportunities for my son, showing my son work ethics and demonstrating that he, too, can discover a deep passion that can become his profession.

Resilience is a practised attitude, so in order to develop, broaden and sustain it, we need to build and evolve new habits that support it and remove old habits that obstruct or deplete our resilience and potential.

5. How we see ourselves

Elizabeth

Elizabeth is one of the most accomplished people I know. As a young, powerful, senior executive, she has become accustomed to being exceptional. When I would listen to her speak, I could hear the depth of her awareness of self and others.

Despite her successes, Elizabeth became unstuck following the birth of her first child. As her son grew, so did her love for him, but this love grew in sync with deep sadness that often morphed into self-doubt. Memories began creeping in that made her feel like she didn't have the skills she needed to be a good parent. After all, the love, stability, attention, care and patience she wanted to give her son were things she'd never known in her own childhood.

She'd learned to breathe through the beatings that her mum once described as 'just a couple of slaps'. The name-calling hit the hardest. The verbal and emotional abuse was so incessant that Elizabeth began to believe she deserved to be treated that poorly, that there was something fundamentally wrong with her.

The offensive behaviours stung more when they were delivered in front of others. Because they'd witnessed the abuse she'd endured, Elizabeth grew more concerned about her neighbours' feelings than the pain or the betrayal that resulted from her mother's abuse.

Some years later, Elizabeth tried to confront her family with the truth of what she'd experienced in her childhood. She was met with even greater brutality, this time delivered indirectly. At first she was ridiculed, then she was scapegoated and ostracised.

As time went on, Elizabeth chose to share as little as possible about her life with her family. Graduations, first days at work and promotions were never shared. She didn't even tell them about the birth of her son until a week later. She knew no one deserved to be treated like she had been, yet Elizabeth felt a deep sense of shame and of not being worthy of love. As a result, she kept trying to prove herself as worthy to others and to her harshest critic – herself.

Although she acted as if she was confident, she was paralysed by social anxiety. She understood the concept of generating greater resilience through the practice of feeling abundant and worthy, but Elizabeth's relationship with her past made this practice close to impossible.

She thought that her motivation for pursuing the goals and ambitions she had nurtured was so that she could change the world for the better. Later, she realised she'd been doing it all to try to gain approval.

After some years had passed, Elizabeth felt this painful discourse in her life was under control. She had done so much good for others and achieved greatly, so she felt as if she had bought her way into being worthy of respect.

However, she found herself coming unstuck at the most unlikely time. A mihi whakatau – a traditional Māori welcoming speech – was being given for a new member of Elizabeth's senior management team. The loved ones of Elizabeth's new member were invited to participate in the mihi whakatau.

When she welcomed the new staff member's family to the conference room prior to the event, Elizabeth was astonished to see two dozen family members, who had travelled from all around the country to provide their support.

The ceremony was beautifully sequenced yet free-flowing, filled with love, warmth and sincerity. Time was not important. Demonstrating utmost respect and deepest appreciation for that family member was what mattered. The family made speeches in which they described Elizabeth's new team member as their taonga – their treasure.

Elizabeth could see how deeply this family knew and appreciated each other. As they were leaving, one member of the family approached Elizabeth with advice on how to lead her new team member: 'If she embraces you, let her. She will never let you down.'

Elizabeth was not ashamed to feel tears flowing down her face. In the past, she might have wondered, 'Why am I not worthy of this love from my own family?' But now she knew that this was not a question for her to answer. Instead, she felt charged and elated by the love she knew she was going to create for those around her.

* * *

Have you heard the saying, 'The map is not the territory'? Like Elizabeth, we all have had challenging experiences. Some of these, when unattended, can restrict the scope of our resilience or deplete us.

The markers on the map are less important than the way in which you choose to traverse the actual ground those markers depict. Your exposures – the starting point, the twists and the turns on your map – don't matter anywhere near as much as the way you choose to navigate them.

Moreover, every experience we have remains a part of the fabric of our life. It is up to us to decide if it will become a valuable lesson, a stepping stone to better things or a poorly disguised trauma. Resilience is often a choice and choice requires engagement, deliberate decisions, capacity to question and exploration. Select and stick to your chosen course of action.

Think, feel, act resiliently

The most powerful intervening factor between an event and an outcome is your choice. To change your patterns and thereby your experience of life you need to think differently. If you notice yourself stuck in a sub-optimal pattern, ask yourself:

- Can I think differently about what is happening? If so, how?
- Can thinking differently support me in feeling differently? If so, how?
- Can I act differently with what is happening as my backdrop?

If you can answer 'yes' to these questions, the challenge is to come up with better responses that you can write into the story of your life. You might feel constrained by the patterns of life you've experienced, by what you perceive to be yours and other's roles in the outcomes you contemplate or see as fixed in time.

This is where blame and ownership can kick in. You might feel a sense of emotional entanglement or a sense of rigidity around what has happened in your life. It might seem as though the décor is changing around you and the backdrop is shifting while the characters influencing you are not changing at all.

The key to moving through this is having the discipline to question yourself and to begin to notice the different opportunities you have to create positive shifts within yourself.

The book of your life

Our memories influence our future behaviours, especially when they involve how other people relate to us. This is especially the case with family relationships, or other close relationships with people who have influenced us strongly.

We all collect memories and experiences, some of which we choose as the foundations of who we are. Then we attribute them with seemingly irremovable labels. Many of us are also shaped, consciously or otherwise, by other people's interpretations of us and the stories we think others create about us – what we think they think we think we are. Fleeting moments in our lives – often poorly coloured by other people's biases, values and views – can lead us to becoming the crumpled vision we think someone else has of us.

Life may start your story with a few tricky lines. Many of us are given chapters that are hard to integrate our hopes for life into. When this happens, we often find ourselves reliving stories that have been handed to us by others. It doesn't have to be like this, though. You can choose your story and change the script. It is up to you whether you will constrain the rest of your life or grow. It is your choice as to how you want to complete each sentence and each page in the book of your life.

We belong in the narrative of our own life, so choose the words you write it with carefully. Choose the colour and the font on your pages. Set your own margins.

Two monks and a woman

Elizabeth's story of letting go is not unique. It is a tale that has been told for as long as words have been spoken. Let me tell you a Buddhist parable of letting go.

Once upon a time, two monks were travelling together on foot when they came upon a powerful river with rapids and choppy waters. As they paused to consider their next move, they noticed a woman standing beside the river, unable to cross it by herself.

Even though the monks had taken a sacred vow never to touch a woman, the elder monk picked the woman up and carried her across the river on his back. Safely on the other side of the river, the monk set the woman down, waited for his companion then quietly continued on his journey.

Hours passed before the younger monk finally asked, 'Why did you carry that woman when we've taken a vow never to touch women?'

His companion replied, 'I set the woman down hours ago by the river. Why are you still carrying her?'

Ask yourself, who or what are you carrying on your back long after you have crossed the rapids of a trial?

Letting go may be the start of your essential journey to resilience. Accepting that you have a choice and then choosing how to change the trajectory of your life for the better is the rest of it. Either way, the choice is yours! You can decide whether to continue to endure the pain of what has passed, thereby fuelling your own hesitance to take the next step towards your goal, or you can choose to push past the obstacles in order to experience whatever you hoped life could offer you.

Depending on how we experience, interpret and store them, memories can continue to infuse their influence in our lives, no matter how long they have been with us. Memories can be remarkably influential in how you choose to respond in the here and now and in the patterns you choose for yourself in the future. They are the well-walked route that you take habitually.

Uninterrupted, our memories can demand that we choose the familiar over the optimal, even when they are at an equal distance from us. Choosing the familiar allows us to take the easy way out, but if what you observe or experience stands in contrast to what you hope for, then perpetuating it is a matter of laziness.

Logically, most of us understand that we should not let a single incident, one bad day or even a series of bad days reduce the rest of our life or change our sense of who we are. Likewise, most of us know the difference between 'I did something bad' and 'I am a bad person', or 'I can grow stronger' and 'I am a weak person', or 'She said she no longer loves me' and

'I am an unlovable person'. However, sometimes when we feel overwhelmed, logic goes out the window.

Survivors and thrivers can feel overwhelmed and even devastated. Resilience allows them to recognise and accept that an event, an emotion or a feeling does not need to take over their entire life.

Feelings can change, evolve and transform us. If we are willing, we can expend our interpretation or relationship with past negative events and allow room for them to help us grow. Much of our life is the sum total of the thoughts and feelings that we entertain. Our identities are less the products of our context and experiences and more the outcome of the stories we tell ourselves, the beliefs we develop about ourselves and our world.

Tool: 30 seconds without leaving the page

What are the stories you tell yourself about yourself based on your current experiences? What is the self-image you chose to belong to? Notice those stories. Choose how you shape them, because they can shape you.

In the spaces below, complete each line in turn as quickly as you can without leaving the page. Don't overthink things. Take note of your first response.

I always ...	People are ...
I never ...	I must ...
I can't ...	I should ...
I can ...	Life is ...
I am ...	My life is ...

Note that if you did this exercise on a good day, it may sound a little like this:

I always ... *succeed*	People are ... *just so great!*
I never ... *give up*	I must ... *high-5 myself even more often*
I can't ... *believe how awesome I am*	I should ... *teach others how to be great*
I can ... *do anything*	Life is ... *wonderful always*
I am ... *amazing*	My life is ... *extraordinary*

A bad day may present a completely different picture:

I always ... *struggle to*	People are ... *untrustworthy*
I never ... *quite make it*	I must ... *keep my guard up even more*
I can't ... *handle pressure*	I should ... *work harder and push myself even more*
I can ... *always find a reason to quit on my dreams*	Life is ... *a drag*
I am ... *a quitter*	My life is ... *so difficult*

Mind the stories you tell yourself. Keep the narratives you want to shape your life.

The rock under the willow tree

In my mind, the smell of lavender essence will forever be associated with some of the safest and happiest moments of my childhood. In an instant, when I smell lavender, I can conjure up crisply ironed, clean linens – decades old, but so loved – in the holiday home of my godmother. Her house was a mere 300 metres away from my family home, yet it could have been on another planet.

Her tiny home was almost entirely furnished with old, well-lived in and loved pieces. Her garden was small and always carefully maintained, so that every season showed respect to what nature would deliver. The creaky steps and the smell of wood, enhanced by the ever-busy termites, meant her home was an ecosystem of its own.

Special meals there included small amounts of delightful delicacies carefully chosen to celebrate the occasion of 'life being shared'. There was always attention, time and space allowed for discussions to emerge, thereby enhancing the experience of life shared. These conversations usually occurred alongside some sort of practical activity, like getting the kindling ready for the fire, making preserves or readying the veggie plot for planting.

There was always something to be done – a job that brought a sense of comfort, continuation, purpose, a sense of control. Be that preparing preserves from the just-picked pears, cleaning the walnuts we'd be given by the neighbours or mending the old rugs so that they might have another decade on the floors of her remarkable home.

Every corner of the house was home to something that held a unique place in the family's history. The value of each of these pieces was not determined by its financial worth or even its practicality, but by the stories that had enveloped them over time. There were always just the two of us in this home – my god mum and me – but I always felt like we were wrapped up in the warm embrace of generations.

This was a home of love, of memories, of belonging. Stories were told about where these pieces had come from, the lives they'd shared and the paths they'd taken to be here.

It was here I learned the importance of antiques. I asked my god mum why she valued old pieces so much and why she didn't seem to care for new things: 'Ah, but these pieces have history, they have a heart.' This helped to focus me on the emotions that history evokes.

This wasn't my permanent home, but I had things in it that made me a part of it, like my own nightgown. It was one my god mum had owned when she was 14, and it had become mine 30 years later. Whenever I went to this home, the nightgown would always be ready on my bed.

Many years later, it dawned on me that the deep conversations I had with my godmother as we did practical tasks were not her preferred modus operandi. Instead, they were a way in which she was trying to heal me from what she felt I carried. As well as providing me with new experiences, and with the utmost of care, she wanted to change the context for my thoughts and reflections. She wanted to create a sense of safety for me that would allow me to create a place to feel at peace within my memories, so that I could find a better place for me in my future.

The human memory works by taking us to a place in time when that piece of memory was established as a part of our identity. She'd made me a part of this place not just so that she could provide me with advice in a way I could absorb it, but also so that I could use the memories I made there as part of my identity and for my growth in the future. She made her home a place where I would always know I belong – then she took that a step further.

In her home, I was never alone. It was a place I could walk my mind back to through the corridors of my memory to find a place for conversations that enabled the best in me. She wanted me to know a place where I could recognise and hear my own thoughts.

One day, she challenged me to identify that one place that I could call my own, where I could sit alone with my thoughts knowing that I had all I needed in myself. Just down the road where the two rivers met was a large boulder that stood in the shade of a willow tree. I could imagine generations of shepherds sitting on that boulder, children and old people cooling off in the shadow of that willow tree. I knew that my place was on that rock under that willow tree.

Re-anchoring

When we are able to consciously ground ourselves and connect with the place where we feel an innate sense of enabling belonging, this can re-anchor us. To do this, we need to draw on and connect with what grounds us, the memories we have that allow us to see ourselves as capable and worthy, and the tools we have readily available to us. If we are able to re-anchor ourselves during or following significant trials, we can then respond to them with a fuller, stronger, more authentic version of ourselves. This can be a memory of a place or a place we have constructed in our minds through meditation and visualisation.

The goal of re-anchoring is to ground you so that you can engage with your environment deliberately rather than reactively or mindlessly. It allows you to engage in the now with a view towards the legacy you want to leave and the emotional tone you wish to evoke through the process of your engagement.

Positive or enabling belonging predicts the degree to which we are willing and able to access our capabilities and how effectively we commit to our potential.

Such a feeling of belonging will fuel the best in you. It will enable you to take purposeful action because it provides an innate sense of safety. It will also help sponsor creativity. The awareness gained from the process of re-anchoring allows you to effectively orient yourself towards opportunity instead of fear.

Tool: Choose your place

Whether you are calling upon the memories of your own version of the rock under the willow or creating one in your mind, this visualisation technique is designed to relax and ground you. From this more relaxed and grounded state, you will be able to make better decisions, better regulate your emotions and increase your resilience repertoire.

- *Find a safe, comfortable place where you will not be interrupted. Lie or sit in a comfortable position and close your eyes.*
- *Slowly walk yourself to a quiet place in your mind. This can be a place you have been or one you build in your mind.*
- *Allow yourself to feel at peace and safe here. Unload your anxieties and worries. For now, your only task is to focus on this space you are creating or bringing back to mind.*
- *What do you see around you in this place? What are the smells, sounds and views you notice? What do you see in the distance? Smell it, hear it, feel it.*
- *Look around for a special spot in this place. Find the best path to that spot. Imagine you can feel the ground beneath your feet as you are moving towards that special spot. What does the ground feel like? Is it a beautiful warm sand, a dewy grass or a soft, comfortable carpet? Keep your attention on what you hear, feel and smell as you move to your special place.*

- *You have arrived at your special place. Take a look around. What does it feel like being there? What do you notice? Reach and touch something in that place in your mind. What does it feel like?*
- *Sit or lie down at this special place. Bring anything you need to be completely comfortable here. Continue to relax into it, noticing how the light shifts and changes around you. Notice the smells and sounds. Notice your feelings. This is your safe place. If danger is here you can expel it. Spend 3–5 minutes noticing the feeling of being safe, relaxed and comfortable. Appreciate the view, touch what is around you, keep absorbing the sounds in this place.*
- *Memorise the smells, sights, sounds, feelings of this place. You can come back here anytime.*
- *When you are ready, leave by the same path you entered. As you are leaving, take note of all the details that this space offers to your senses of sight, hearing, smell and touch.*
- *Say an affirmation such as, 'This is my place and I can come here whenever I please.'*

Bartering with faith

We seek patterns to help us feel like we can predict life –
good, bad or otherwise. Familiar patterns are easier for us
to opt into even when they hold us back. Most of us become
experts in bartering with faith, which happens when we know
things can be better but we find it easier to remain within
familiar patterns.

Bartering with faith never leads to a meaningful result. Its
the sound of 'If … then …' It is something most of us hear
daily: 'I am not happy with this, but I have to keep handling it
because it is what I know. *If* [one element] changes *then* I will
commit myself to changing, too.'

'If … then …' only works in simple, tightly controlled
conditions. For example: 'If I drop my toast, then the buttered
side will hit the ground.' (Apparently, the toast will not
inevitably land buttered side down. It does so only because we
usually place the toast butter side up and have similar height
tables. Change the height of the fall and the speed of rotation
and the odds may change.)

Life is seldom simple or as easily controlled as buttered toast.
Most of us deplete our resilience before even testing it, as we
work on the premise of Murphy's law: anything that can go
wrong will go wrong. Working on this basis, we are choosing
to ignore all the factors that can interfere with this equation –
the most important one being ourselves! Rather than worrying

about things we have no control or influence over, we can create the conditions we need to thrive. As my entrepreneurial friend Khan once said: 'I have the best conditions because I create the best conditions.' Then he added: 'Don't excuse yourself with your circumstances. Find the circumstances you need. If you can't find them, create them.'

How will you break away from yet another shade of the usual to broaden and build your resilience?

Belonging beyond self

In my interviews with members of the SAS, their message was clear:

> To engage effectively with challenges and thrive in ambiguity, you must have the resources to step forward from a place of strength rather than a place of fear, perceived deprivation or scarcity. Belonging is an essential, precious resource in this.

The SAS are selected and trained to be self-reliant, to be capable of operating in relative isolation, yet one of the crucial pillars for their resilience is belonging. That surprised me.

When thinking of the self-reliance that SAS members are expected to display, the image of Baron Munchhausen always emerges in my mind. Munchhausen is a fictional character who (often clumsily) pursues purpose and adventure. Such is Baron Munchhausen's self-reliance that he once pulled himself and the horse he was sitting on out of a swamp by his own hair. Defeating gravity is one thing, but expecting that we can be resilient when we don't feel like we belong? That's near impossible.

Belonging is a universal need and one that is fundamental for resilience. However, there are caveats to the sorts of belonging that fuels our resilience.

It is only in the full awareness of ourselves, of the stuff that makes us authentically us and the nuances we carry from our lessons learned, that we can make space to belong.

The survivors and thrivers often refer to their sense of belonging, chiefly as it is essential for their ability to thrive in ambiguity.

The kind of belonging worth keeping is what they refer to as 'enabling' belonging. Enabling belonging serves to replenish you no matter whether its source is physically proximate or geographically or temporally removed.

Enabling belonging is like a well of faith in a drought. When you have been under an onslaught of pressure for too long you can begin to wonder, 'Can I deal with this? Am I a worthy human?' In such times, just the memory of what you mean to trusted others, their perception of you, their expectations of and hopes for you can drive you and sustain your resilience beyond your wildest dreams.

Another survivor and thriver warns us though that not all wells are made equal and that we need to make conscious choices about where we commit our trust.

Belonging is fundamentally about trust, and in the context of thriving, predictability makes up only a small part of that trust.

Trust-to-belong demands unapologetic judgement on the competence, integrity and benevolence of the 'space' we choose to belong to. It begs the questions:

- Will this space see me at my best?
- Does it aim to see me at my best?
- Can it serve as my vital lifeline and as my platform so I can contribute at my best?

A gang, a coffee group or a dysfunctional family

You are where you choose to belong, so be careful of the voices you choose to listen to. Perhaps your grandma told you, 'Mind the company you are keeping. It becomes you.'

You may think you belong to a gang, a coffee club or a dysfunctional family. Each of these may have a way of supporting belonging for resilience in some way, for some time. However, belonging for resilience is less about our habits, hobbies, thrill of escape or a place in a family tree designated by birth.

Survivors and thrivers choose where they belong, in the fullness of their capabilities, knowing this belonging serves to see them, as one of my SAS interviewees said, 'Bigger than just themselves, stronger than they would be on their own and committed to protect and grow capacity for contribution that may otherwise demand superhuman capabilities.'

A strong sense of belonging serves as a powerful pillar for resilience in times of trial, even when we are physically removed from our respective sources of belonging or support. For some, resilience will be linked to a sense of belonging to their organic family; for others, it will stretch beyond family to a sense of cultural or community belonging or shared faith.

Tool: Your reference for belonging

Reflect on your own reference to belonging and list whatever comes to mind first. It could be your workplace, immediate and extended family, cultural or social group. Reflect on as many references as appear to captivate your sense of belonging for yourself. Consider each in turn. Now consider your responses to the following question and prompts. Every one of these prompts is important for enabling belonging.

Does this place or these people you feel you belong to:

- *fuel or deplete you?*
- *strengthen or erode your confidence?*
- *grow or decimate your hope?*
- *propel or paralyse your vision?*
- *evolve or stunt your growth?*

I hope that your references to belonging fuel, strengthen, grow, propel and evolve you. If the opposite is true in some or all of the prompts, then it is time to consider your membership of those groups or places. Indeed, this is what Elizabeth did in order to rebuild her resilience. After a decade of careful thought, introspection and professional support, she had to decide that her relationship with her mother was toxic and she needed to remove herself from it. However, we don't always have to divorce our families or quit our social groups if they don't fit the positive side of belonging all of the time.

The reality is that there may be in-between times when we may describe our sense of belonging to people or places with terms like 'on the one hand ... and on the other hand ...' For example, on the one hand, my beautiful son fuels me with immense joy and purpose, but on the other hand, as a lively seven-year-old, he also depletes me.

When in these in-between places, the challenge is to reflect on how you navigate your relationship of belonging mindfully, meaningfully and constructively. This means you need to study and adapt the way you engage with belonging so that it sustains your resilience even when the very source of it may be your challenge.

6. See it in your mind

Maria

Growing up in Sofia, my springboard diving coach Maria was a force to be reckoned with – frightening and loveable in equal measure.

When we committed to executing a new jump or a movement, Maria would tell us to visualise what it would look like with as much detail and in the most effective sequence we could imagine. She'd then get us to practise the move in our minds repeatedly before we ever got to test it in the pool. She would always say to us: 'See it in your mind first. See it clearly and the body will follow.'

I doubt Maria had ever had any theoretical training in visualisation, she just intuitively knew the importance of it and she had a way of demonstrating its impact practically and in the moment.

She'd challenge us to make space in our minds to envision being better. She wanted us to step in with the belief that complex tasks were possible in our minds before we committed our bodies to them. Inevitably, she was right.

Whenever I tried to execute a new move without mental preparation or when I was feeling overwhelmed by fear or incompetence, my body would carry out an outdated iteration of the move. If I practised the move in my mind in rich detail and in sequence, somehow my muscles were better prepared to follow that same sequence in the pool.

Maria was also a mind reader. She was somehow able to tell when our minds weren't fully present and focused on the task at hand. One day, she showed up at the pool with a bag of rubber bands for each of the diving squad members. At first, I thought they were for tying our hair back, but then she gave them to everyone, irrespective of their hair length.

She made us put these bands on our wrists and use them to remind us to be where our bodies were – where our feet were – every time our brains wandered away from the pool or the movement we were about to execute. If we found ourselves distracted from the task at hand, we would just flick the rubber band on our wrists. Being present in the moment mattered. Being grounded and belonging fully to our intent, to how we wanted to tackle the challenge, was the next step.

When I first started training, I'd show up to the pool full of anxiety. Soon, no matter how demanding Maria was, that time in the pool became the most anticipated part of my day. The joy of executing complex jumps to the best of my ability was hugely satisfying.

Before long, I realised that Maria's teachings were translating across other aspects of my life – school, socialising, building my ideas for my future. Time in the pool offered a whole lot more than training physical moves. The fall I'd worried about hadn't happened. Once I'd set my mind on how I wanted things to turn out, my body knew the plan it had to follow.

In winter, I'd put plastic rubbish bags over my socks to slow the inevitable soaking of my feet as I walked to the pool from my family's apartment. One day, I told Maria my toes were still frozen from my walk to the pool.

Maria always showed up to the pool in immaculate training gear. Then one day, she arrived and her pants were wet. She didn't own a washing machine and the water to her house had been disconnected some time ago, so she had to do her washing at an outdoor sink then hang it in the sun to dry.

She had hoped that the winter sun would dry her washing more effectively than her unheated house in the middle of winter, but not even the sun had the power to dry her clothes outside of the hours she was needed at the pool.

In spite of all that, she willed herself to live for her purpose of training the future generation of springboard divers at a cost that couldn't compare to one day of frozen toes for me.

Maria deserved the utmost respect for being our coach. Not only had she achieved at the highest levels in the sport as an athlete herself, but she sacrificed a lot to be there as our coach decades later. Sport had lost funding in post-communist Bulgaria and Maria was not paid for the work she did. So that she could afford to train us, she did two jobs, one of which was as the pool cleaner – a job she did around our training sessions.

She always told us, 'Whatever is possible for your mind is possible for your life.' However hard her life was, Maria left no doubt that she belonged in the fullness of her self.

Tool: Belong in the now

Stress, worry, self-defeating thoughts and anxiety can yank you out of your opportunity in the present moment. It is as if, suddenly, there is a thick glass wall between where you are and where you want to be. You can see where you want to be, but you cannot reach it.

You may have been preparing to take a leap towards better for some time, but in the decisive moment you find that negative thoughts prevent you from doing it. Here are three exercises to help you take control of such moments.

'Stop!'
When you notice negative thoughts in your mind, imagine yourself shouting 'Stop!' Imagine hearing your voice speaking with authority and confidence. If saying or shouting 'Stop!' in your head doesn't stop the negative thought, put a rubber band around your wrist and snap it as you shout 'Stop!' to yourself.

Belly breathing
Focus on your breathing. Ensure you take deep, long breaths from your belly. Guide your breathing by placing one hand on your belly and one on your chest. Watch as your belly rises as you breathe in and sinks as you breathe out.

Start counting your breaths as you exhale. Empty your mind. Once you've counted four deep exhales, start again from one. Continue this until you feel relaxed. Repeat this exercise whenever negative thoughts take up space in your mind.

Change channels

Bring to mind a significant achievement or a positive milestone, or cast your mind to a place and time that you anticipate enjoying in the future. Get the emotions associated with this positive image or memory clear in your mind. Engage all senses.

If visualising is difficult for you, disrupt the negative flow of the experience. Go for a run or a walk, play your favourite soundtrack, look at a cherished image of your life that brings you joy. Whatever it is that you do, the aim is to dislodge the negative stream of thought long enough for you to realise you have control over what occupies your mental space.

Select and repeat a coping mantra, such as 'I am capable', 'I am safe', 'I am able' or 'I do hard things'. Choose your own mantra and repeat it as many times as it takes for you to notice you can, once again, see yourself as willing to move forward.

Old habits

If you live your purpose and commit to it with full intention, nothing will exceed your capacity. Pressure is supposed to fuel, stretch, grow and regenerate you – not deplete you. Pressure is the language of your cells. What depletes you is your attitude to pressure.

Most of us spend our time in places, both physically and in our minds, that are familiar. We revisit them, even when we realise they are not the best places for us to occupy. We play a part in the habitual even when we know it is far from our optimal. Our brains love the familiar, especially when under pressure. While most of us can envision better ways of being, we get drawn back into the habitual. Selecting and committing to better habits is a common challenge. When addressing students at the University of Florida in 1998, American business magnate and philanthropist Warren Buffett said:

> Chains of habit are too light to be felt, until they become too heavy to be broken.

We all have readily available switches, built by habits, that are familiar. We use these switches when – having developed the awareness that we could do, feel, think or act better – we need an out, so we act out of habit instead. The most common switch is one I've labelled 'maybe tomorrow'.

- Maybe tomorrow I will feel strong enough to have that conversation.

- Maybe tomorrow I will commit to developing the skills I need to take that next step.
- Maybe tomorrow someone will step up and give me the freedom to do what I know I should be doing.
- Maybe tomorrow I will be better off financially so I'll be able to focus on my health/loved ones/passions.

All of these 'maybes' are riddled with old narratives and biases that prevent us from standing firm on our feet, with our eyes, minds and hearts wide open. Maybe tomorrow will work, but probably not. Resilience is best developed and broadened in the now. Maybe tomorrow is a slippery timeline that tends to shift unless we act on our commitment.

Resilience is conditioned when we anticipate the discomfort that comes with building new habits and commit to change anyway.

Habits are a redundant set of automatic, unconscious thoughts, behaviours and emotions that are acquired through repetition. Whether resilience-enabling or resilience-depleting, our thoughts and behaviours are often habitual. Our bodies become habituated to the most common thoughts and behaviours, even when they are not optimal, because these are more easily accessible. Our bodies activate the habitual faster than our minds can select the optimal.

Memories cue us to make predictions about how our day will unfold, based on the associations we've made with the people and experiences we think we will encounter. As a result, the vast majority of us start our new days in the moments of yesterday. We try to start the new but continuously re-enact our past.

In the words of Buck Owens, the American musician, singer, song writer and band leader: 'I am who I am, I am what I am, I do what I do and I ain't never gonna do it any different.'

You may recognise these words as the voice of the habits that pull you away from your resilience. I will not judge Buck's words without their context. However, in the context of resilience, these are the opposite of what we are after. They highlight stubbornness and perhaps grit, and they are contrary to resilience.

Resilience demands openness to change for the better, but the memory of who you were yesterday sometimes gets in the way of who you might become today.

How you feel is typically influenced by the memories you evoke and the emotions you habitually select for these memories or that you contribute to new experiences.

Unless we deliberately select, envision and move towards our intent, the familiar past will become the predictable future sooner or later. Every tiny action and routine we repeat habituates a set of thoughts and feelings, which then influence our actions.

When we try to do something new from a place of anxiety, the ways we think and feel determine the actions available for us to take. Suddenly, in spite of our better hopes, we belong in the exact version of yesterday that we had hoped we'd bounce away from today. Instead, in order for us to build, broaden and sustain greater resilience, our actions and routines need to be aligned with our goals.

We often register the need to be more resilient in a moment of passing awareness, a dreamlike state that allows us to contemplate better options for our lives. We may envisage this better version of ourselves when comparing ourselves to others, or when we accept that the weight in our ways of being, thinking, feeling and acting is too heavy to carry on with.

You cannot disrupt habitual behaviours with thought alone. You need actions. As our Olympian said, 'It takes vision *and* sweat.'

You need to be clear on what matters more than the habits that deplete you and make those things the immovable stepping stones towards your future, reinforce the better habits and reward your commitment to integrating them into your script for life. Meditation and mindfulness can help us do this.

Meditation and mindfulness

Practising meditation and mindfulness can help us get beyond the analytical mind. The practice of belonging in the moment will help you learn that you don't need to be affected by every passing thought, memory or prediction that your mind makes. Meditation and mindfulness also disrupt the habitual by helping you realise that you don't need to engage with anything other than the thoughts, feelings and emotions that are aligned with your intent.

They also help you to slow down enough to enter a state where you can begin to make some really important changes in the moment. Slowing down the habitual so you can select the optimal is a critical skill for resilience. It allows us to gain greater access to a state of calm composure.

Start with tiny habits

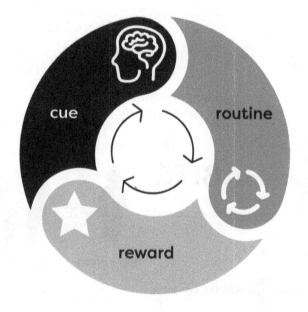

The intensity of the emotion we feel bounds us chemically and neurologically to events in our lives and to predictions we make for ourselves and our world. If we lock into an experience, a momentary emotion can become a mood, the mood a temperament, and the temperament a personality trait that offers fit or misfit with different interactions during our lives. Thoughts and feelings travel in tandem, bringing in supporting experiences to validate the assumptions we make about the world and our place in it.

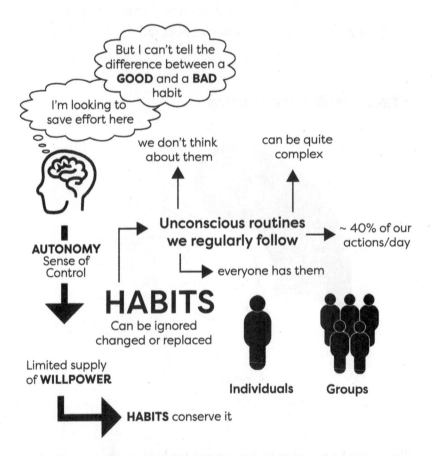

Biologically, more readily accessible thoughts and emotions are the ones that seem to support our survival, the ones that typically come together with a warning sign. They present as a cautionary tale in our lives and re-emerge with a persistent undertone. They offer an invitation to worry and ruminate and expect us to locate a reason to do so. How this process works in our cognition is captured by the anecdote of the 'proactive' mother, who sends a message to her son that reads: 'Start worrying son. Details to follow.'

When working to condition resilience, these are the equivalent of wanting to execute a perfect springboard jump with nothing but the memory of your worst attempt replaying in your mind.

Our bodies don't know the difference between the experiences that create the emotion and the emotion that you're creating in your thoughts.

The hardest part about change is choosing not to make the same suboptimal choice you made the day before. Then to make that better choice over and over again, until the optimal becomes the habit that carries you through.

- What thoughts do you want to carry and perpetuate in your mind?
- What behaviours do you want to demonstrate?

Resilience lies in choosing the habits to belong to, selecting the rituals, routines and habituating the thoughts, actions and feelings that support a better version of life.

Resilience is conditioned in your daily actions. You can habituate resilience every time you act in a way that will help you reach your goal. When you align routines and habits, you turn the optimal into a more readily available script, one that your mind can opt into with greater confidence.

Tool: Your values journey

This is a part of a powerful exercise called 'Your values journey'. I have used this same exercise with a remarkable organisation called Impact International, who are committed to unleashing potential in the global top talent. You might consider going for a walk as you do this exercise, pausing to reflect and take notes on each of the tasks, listening to your favourite sounds as you go. Complete each task in turn and enjoy the journey.

Task 1: Defining your values

On this list of values, circle the 20 that jump out because of their importance to you. If there's something that's important to you missing from the list, add it.

Uniqueness	Family	Generosity	Courage	Trust
Spirituality	Open-mindedness	Humility	Cooperation	Relationships
Reliability	Achievement/Success	Community support	Curiosity	Persistence/Determination
Knowledge	Transparency	Love	Prudence	Purpose
Faith	Accountability	Compassion	Dignity	Simplicity
Growth	Flexibility	Integrity	Justice	Peace
Hope	Freedom	Appreciation	Recognition	Work/life balance
Commitment	Honesty	Vitality	Prosperity	Zest
Responsiveness	Fulfillment	Legacy	Humour	Self-control
Success	Happiness	Support	Sincerity	Freedom
Loyalty	Fun	Recognition	Focus	Resourceful
Hard work	Cleverness	Wisdom	Friendship	Other

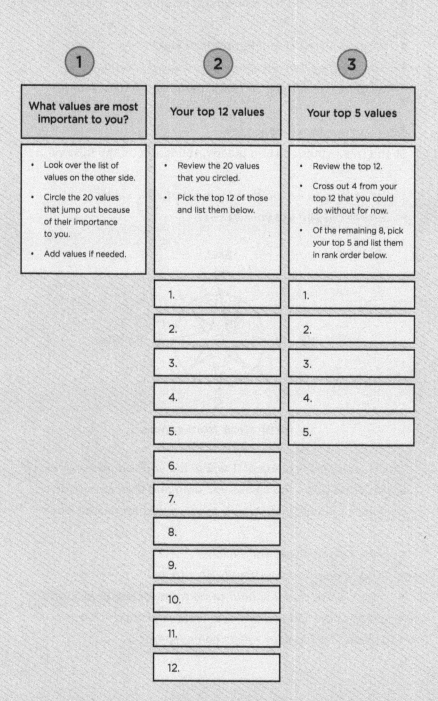

1

What values are most important to you?

- Look over the list of values on the other side.
- Circle the 20 values that jump out because of their importance to you.
- Add values if needed.

2

Your top 12 values

- Review the 20 values that you circled.
- Pick the top 12 of those and list them below.

1.

2.

3.

4.

5.

6.

7.

8.

9.

10.

11.

12.

3

Your top 5 values

- Review the top 12.
- Cross out 4 from your top 12 that you could do without for now.
- Of the remaining 8, pick your top 5 and list them in rank order below.

1.

2.

3.

4.

5.

Task 2: Reflective journey part 1

Notice and really appreciate where you are now and how you got here. Reflect on the following questions:

- *Why are your values important to you?*
- *How do they influence your actions and your life?*
- *What values are you currently demonstrating in your life?*

Task 3: Your inner compass

Spend five minutes sitting quietly, reflecting on the following:

- *What influenced the development of your values?*
- *Where did you get your values?*

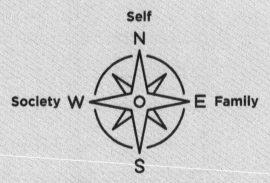

Inspiration from others

This is your inner compass. It will guide you towards your true north. Write down the values you hold and then answer these questions to investigate where those values originated from.

- *Who helped shape your values?*
- *What values did your family give to you?*
- *What values that you hold came from society or inspiration?*
- *What values did you discover were important for yourself?*
- *Where else did your values come from?*

Task 4: Reflective journey part 2

The next page has a blank space for you to draw the outline of your body – your whole body.

Don't worry, this isn't a drawing competition! Please add some identifying features like your face and your hair.

Look at your compass and your own outline and ask yourself honestly, do they match up? Do you travel through life true to your values compass?

In our society, there is a phenomenon called the values gap. By this we mean that sometimes people find they are required (or think they're required) to compromise their personal values to achieve some other goal. There is little emphasis (sometimes none at all) in society on travelling down the often-difficult road of upholding one's values. This reward is internal.

This is a contentious and difficult issue that many people struggle with every day. The concept of bridging the values gap addresses this issue – it urges people to live their values through their actions and to walk the talk.

Reflect on the following:

- *How much are you currently living your five core values?*
- *Are you really the person your compass says you are?*
- *Do you live your values through your actions?*
- *What do you currently do when these values are compromised?*
- *What is the effect of this on you and other significant people within your life? How does this make you feel? Where do you feel it (head, heart, gut, etc.)?*
- *What's holding you back from being true to your compass?*
- *Where are your gaps?*

On your body outline, write and/or draw your gaps based on where you feel these in your body (head, heart, gut, etc.) and reflect on the following:

- *What values do you sometimes compromise? What are the reasons for this?*
- *What role do your saboteurs play in the compromises that you make in living your values?*
- *What are the barriers stopping you from living your values in your actions?*

Task 5: A new map

Take a moment to contemplate the following:

- *Who do you want to be?*
- *What really matters most to you?*

Find a quiet space away from others. Using your body outline and compass as a guide, make yourself a new map of your future. This is the start of an action plan for how you are going to achieve your goals while living true to your inner compass and values. These are the things that will help keep you heading for your true north.

Reflect on the following:

- *Who do you want to be?*
- *What really matters most to you?*
- *How are you going to bridge the gaps?*
- *What are one or two important actions you can take to address the values you are not currently living sufficiently in your life?*

Task 6: Staying on course

Go back to your drawing of your body. Change what you have written on it to symbolise your commitment to bridging these gaps. Reword them. Cross them out. Do whatever is right for you.

The five values you chose are those that are core to your sense of self and your satisfaction/happiness. It's important to ensure these are never compromised, otherwise your resilience will be affected.

We need to know and stay anchored in who we are, in what we value and what we stand for. Our actions may not always reflect our deepest beliefs, but being clear about our values can keep us anchored when things around us might seem to be falling apart.

Our compass will help us to stay on course with our true north. It can keep us in touch with our authentic, resilient and responsible selves, with who we are and, most importantly, with who we want to become.

There will be gaps between our values and our behaviours. Filling those gaps is a constant struggle for everyone. If we don't notice the gaps and strive to fill them by better matching our values and behaviours, chances are we will find little meaning in what we do, no matter how great the external rewards.

If we track our progress and stay on course towards our true north, our values will evolve and mature. We will grow and the growth will be satisfying.

Find somewhere quiet to reflect on the following:

- *What one step do you need to take in the next 24 hours to move in the direction you'd like to head?*
- *Who can support you?*
- *Who will support you?*

After you've finished these reflections, make a note of the following:

- *Which values are you satisfied that you are currently living well?*
- *Which values would you like to live more in order to increase your level of satisfaction?*
- *What do you think is getting in the way of you living these values?*
- *What beliefs/assumptions are associated with these behaviours?*
- *Are these beliefs/assumptions true? How do you know?*
- *What would you have to believe in order to take new/different actions?*

7. Belong and make better

Officer M

Officer M is a member of the global Special Forces community. She has remarkable humility and quite a reputation. The stories surrounding her involve apparent superhuman powers, unshakeable commitment and enviable levels of resilience.

Unlike many soldiers of her generation, Officer M has done as much work as a civilian volunteer as she has in uniform. On several occasions, she has stepped out of uniform to support charity groups around the world. It is her own family background that has seen her develop an unrelenting commitment to help children and those in need.

Her superpower and her vulnerability are one and the same – she never has the patience to stand back and wait for the international community to get into gear when disaster hits. Instead, she is one of the first on the ground and she's committed to living her life in service to whoever needs her most: 'Once I know there is a need, my mind goes instantly into exploring, wondering, contemplating ways to change things, if only slightly, for as many people as I can. I know I can always find something to shift. A tiny shift, even if it is a moment of hope for those who may have lost it all – that's my highest reward and I am willing to pay any price for it. A shift, however tiny or short lived, can have an exponential impact. There is nothing greater.'

Officer M's eyes look younger than her age, as they are filled with hope, determination and joy. This alone seems an odd and unlikely fit for someone who volunteers to serve in the environments in which she has spent her life. She has a restless leg, which bounces while her gaze is fixed firmly and calmly on whoever she speaks to. It is as if, no matter how committed Officer M is to the conversation, her body is ready to react to a crisis she knows she can prevent from escalating. She is in a constant sense of readiness with an utter sense of clarity.

Officer M has the sort of presence that would transform even the dingiest room into a space worth cherishing, celebrating and respecting. She always shows up in her best, as if to demonstrate the commitment she has made to this moment in time.

Like most members of this community, Officer M seems to have an elevated appreciation for life. After all, they've signed themselves up for the possibility of losing their life in the pursuit of something greater than themselves.

Not only has she overcome some of the most complex challenges any person could survive, but she is also joyful, grateful and full of life and hope. Rather than talking about past hardships, she prefers to talk about future opportunities and about giving back.

Everyone she interacts with leaves feeling like they were the worthiest human she could sit with in that moment. With all the experiences and stories that sit in her memory bank, somehow she is always more interested in asking questions of others. The way she listens to their stories leaves them in no doubt that their lives deserve to have books written about them.

When asked how she has maintained her hope and capacity for joy, having chosen to live her life in some of the most treacherous and troubled parts of the world, she replies: 'It is simple. I accept I am unlikely to make a radical difference on my own. My being there will not make things go away. I have long accepted I can't singlehandedly stop world conflict or famine. But I know that I have the skills and the opportunity to take tiny actions that can settle the chaos for a moment.

'If I can reduce pain for someone even for a micro moment every day I get given, then I am good. If I can alleviate the pressure or create an opportunity for just one person for just one day, my life is full. This gives me immense joy; it gives my life purpose. My joy is there because I can and because I choose to take actions daily.'

I asked Officer M what has driven and sustained her to live her life in this way, and she didn't hesitate to answer: 'The layers of complexity and ambiguity we encounter are so many and so thick. They land on you fast. The only gear that you can be in to work through these layers is a sense of adventure, an exploratory mindset and a readiness to adapt every nuance in yourself and your context.

'Curiosity feeds your sense of adventure. If you live your life well, you will achieve one milestone, and before you get the chance to celebrate, you'll discover that there are plenty more goals to be achieved, more good to be done. So, you get there, and you realise you must go a little further – always. You could not handle this constant process of stretching and learning if you were not curious.'

Two lines in particular – 'A shift, however tiny or short lived, can have an exponential impact', and 'My joy is there because I can and because I choose to take actions daily' – have stayed with me. I can and I choose to take action daily. I reflect on this, especially when I know I can, but I have chosen not to take action daily or otherwise. What is in my way that isn't in her way?

Officer M reminded me of Soldier A (see page 36). He shared similar views when he said, 'When you are feeling stuck, commit to improving someone else's lot. Not only will you improve their life, even if for a moment, but you will also regain faith that you have the power to influence life.'

The mandate of 'belong and make better' is this. Resilience is sustained and grows when we find a way to improve our predicament or help those around us.

Be the pivot

Every one of us can be a person of remarkable, positive influence for another. A kind word, a caring gesture or a helping hand can make a world of difference to the recipient of your power to belong in the moment and make it better. It can also contribute directly to your resilience.

Take a moment. Notice. Who can you aid in pivoting to the better right now? Your action can be as little as smiling at a stranger or acknowledging the strengths of a colleague. It can be sending a random note of appreciation to a friend.

However big or small, be the pivot to better, belong in your strength, belong in your potential to improve.

You, the hero

One of the SAS soldiers I interviewed shared with me, 'When you are sleep-deprived, sore and hungry, it is a whole lot easier to cross over an obstacle course with the backdrop of your favourite power soundtrack in your mind.'

While he may have been referring to an actual soundtrack involving cherished music, it meant more than that. To see yourself past the obstacles of life, the soundtrack you play in your mind should contain tales of your past successes and memories of times when you overcame what seemed unsurmountable. By playing those stories in your mind, you are more likely to take on an obstacle with a smile on your face.

Tool: The hero in me

We seldom pause to appreciate the hero in ourselves - our strengths, our uniqueness and our remarkable gifts. We can all improve and do better, always. However, to do our best and thrive, we need to start from a place of strength. Take time and really focus on you. Reflect on the hero in you by answering the following questions:

- *Who is the hero in me?*
- *What drives me and why?*
- *How will I amplify my impact?*
- *Who am I at my best and how do I amplify that while I dampen the rest?*

PART 3
CURIOSITY

8. The importance of curiosity

I owe my life to curiosity. In 2012 I was selected to be one of 120 international UN Military Observers (UNMO) serving across Israel, Lebanon, Jordan, Syria and Egypt.

Early on in my deployment our team was stationed at UN Observation Post 58 near the Syrian village of Al Jamla, perched perfectly between Syria's borders with Israel and Jordan. Tension in the area had been intensifying for some time and we felt somewhat immune to it. Until, in the golden hour of a spring day, we found ourselves stuck in a ferocious crossfire between rebel forces and the Syrian army, and secured ourselves for days in a 1960s, 3 by 5 underground bunker.

For most of our time in the bunker, all we could do was report on what we could hear through the stone walls. At one stage, the main building we would usually occupy received an artillery round, collapsing the concrete roof of our kitchen. We busied ourselves with planning alternative courses of action in case we had a chance to escape. When we exhausted these, we would kick into jokes or outrageous memories to lift our spirits. In reality, the severity of our situation did not became apparent until we left our shelter days later.

As we drove away from Al Jamla, the devastation was confronting. Cows that had been grazing on the fields just days earlier were no longer standing and no longer whole. These animals had been the primary source of sustenance for the families who owned them. They were seen as friends, even family members, never to be abandoned. The devastation was complete; the silence as we drove out was deafening. Did anyone make it alive out of Al Jamla?

Our way out of this predicament was not through a UN diplomatic corridor. Instead, a ceasefire window had been organised by a single UN soldier we had never met but who'd had a conversation with a member of a rebel group at a nearby checkpoint.

The UN soldier had driven past this checkpoint for weeks, wondering about the circumstances that saw the rebels end up there, sheltering in the ruins of a concrete building with a roof fashioned from a tarpaulin and old truck tyres. In Syria, as in all war-torn areas, we never knew when the UN would become a target of aggression. Many saw the UN as ineffectual, detached and blind to the suffering that was taking place around them. You could never be too cautious.

But curiosity prevailed on a cold, rainy day when the UN soldier decided to stop and share his flask of hot coffee with the rebel running the checkpoint. His only intent was to offer a moment of respite to a fellow human stuck out in the rain and the cold.

The two men discovered they were the same age, had the same number of children and were both far from their homes and loved ones in service to a cause greater than themselves. They both hoped that they'd be able to return home safely and they both dreamed of a better future for themselves and their loved ones.

A week later, their accidental and unlikely bond allowed for a short ceasefire to be negotiated, thereby securing our extraction from our obliterated observation post. Our lives had been saved by one man's genuine curiosity.

* * *

Some months later, UN Observation Post 52 had become my home. From there, stationed uncomfortably and (as we thought) safely on the hills above, I had watched the towns of Bariqa and Bi'r al 'Ajam being mercilessly pounded by small arms fire, grenades and artillery fire by the Syrian Army and every other warring party.

For months, we had been there on the hill, equipped with our binoculars to observe and report these devastating events, yet we were powerless to influence or prevent them no matter how diligently we crafted our reports. The feeling of confusion became as familiar as the smells and sounds of the brutal civil war that surrounded us every minute of every day.

Then, one cold night, I was woken by the sound of people breaking into our observation post. Given our remote location, it was unusual to hear voices at night, let alone this many of them. As possibilities started rushing through my mind, I heard my colleague F, who was on duty that night, make a Mayday call from our operations room next door.

My first thought was, 'The UN must be running a training exercise. They are just testing us with the old "shock and awe" approach.'

I had taken part in training exercises in the Australian outback that had begun in much the same way. The aim of these military excercises was to offer a sense of readiness and a frame of reference that would help us process something that initially seemed uncontrollable. Even though carefully designed training excercises were just simulations, they would stop feeling fake the minute a participant would react as if they were real.

Up in OP 52, it soon became apparent that this was not a training drill. Our building was being swarmed by heavily armed militia members. The intruders had crept up the hill on foot so that they could fly under the radar more easily.

We had ways out, but none of them were viable. The Mayday call had alerted UN troops stationed about 15 kilometres away from our post. There was a slim chance of them getting to us in time, but the only way for them to reach us was on roads and through towns that were currently in the crossfire between rebel groups and the Syrian armed forces.

Our own vehicles were sitting right in front of our operations room. The only road to safety would lead us to a gate in the Israeli technical fence – a heavily fortified mesh separating Israel and Syria – less than a kilometre away from our building. On a bad day, when the tension in Syria was high, the gate would be locked. On a good day, that gate would be open and flanked by UN military vehicles. Even if by some miracle we were able to make it past 38 armed military militia members and into our vehicles, our short drive would lead us to a locked gate. We could hear safety, we could see it, we could almost smell it, but we could not reach for it.

That evening, the first thing I noticed when one of the intruders looked through the window into my room was that he was startled to see a female standing there. I found his reaction oddly encouraging. I would have felt more anxious if he had stood and stared at me as I pulled my clothes on. It made me realise that if they had been observing us for any length of time, they would have known there was a female in the mix.

Was he just a random soldier who had been called in at the last minute? Had their briefing not been detailed enough? It was clear that whoever these intruders were, not all of them were on the same page. That had the potential to make them more dangerous, but there was also greater hope that we could influence them. We could try to barter, strike up conversations and build rapport with them much more easily if they were not unified. Our minds were restlessly racing through assumptions just to maintain an illusion of control. Shots were fired.

They had broken into our building. This phase was over. A new phase was about to begin.

When one of the intruders grabbed my wrists, I noticed that the palms of his hands were sweaty even though it was a cold night. I managed to push his hands away, then gestured to him that he should wipe them before he touched me. My assumption that he was nervous created hope and openings.

They had a translator speaking to us from the other side of a window that had been smashed moments earlier. He had a long beard and soft eyes, which made him look like a teacher rather than a terrorist. Then again, what does a terrorist look like? Was he forced to be here against his will? If this was his first task with this group, could this make him more or less dangerous?

As my two UN colleagues – F and N – and I watched on, we noticed one of the intruders directing the others with a great deal more confidence than the rest. He seemed to be watching how everyone responded. Perhaps he was their leader.

Clearly, we had been overpowered. There were three of us and we were unarmed. We'd been taken hostage by 38 heavily armed militia members.

Despite the highly volatile situation we found ourselves in, we continued to gather intelligence. Just the fact that we were studying them gave us a sense of control. Perhaps there was an opportunity for us to influence the larger group and defend ourselves against them?

Our minds were busy studying, painting pictures, building assumptions, developing theories and noticing emotions as – given the opportunity – any of these things could come in handy.

However this was going to play out, I was collecting information to provide detailed feedback to everyone back home about who had taken us hostage. The possibility that I might not make it out alive didn't even cross my mind until much later.

Self-awareness, interpersonal awareness and situational awareness came into focus. In the drive to survive, I became curious about our captors' motivation.

They told us they planned to 'make a bad video' of us. At the time, videos of 'enemies' being decapitated were being uploaded to the internet with alarming regularity as part of the warring parties' propaganda machines. The videos were intended to show commitment and uncompromising purpose and, of course, to intimidate.

If we had stopped to mull over our captors' motivation in the way they had articulated it, we would have had no reason to doubt their intent and every reason to believe we were in a world of trouble!

As soon as we left our observation post, our chances of survival rapidly decreased. I wondered whether, as a female officer, my fate was going to be different from the men. But I had to let fear go. It was of no use. We didn't have time to stop and think about the worst case scenario. We were so absorbed by what was happening right in front of us. Even as the light at the end of the tunnel grew dimmer, we continued to think of ways out of our predicament.

Forced out into the night at gunpoint, the threat was acute. My logical mind told me this would not go well for us and it would hurt in every way.

That very morning, F and I had been training on a concrete platform in the shade. We'd been doing quick sequences of exercises designed to get our bodies to match the strain our minds were under on this mission as 'Mindfields' by The Prodigy was blasting from a nearby speaker. Both F, who was from northern Europe and I, a Bulgarian New Zealander, thought the song was called 'Minefields', which – given our location – seemed appropriate.

Sometime later, as we were being dragged through some nearby minefields, F stole a moment and said to me: 'Buddy! We are doing it for real!'

I smirked. Suddenly, I thought, 'We've got this. We've got one on them, even if it is just for a fleeting moment.' This injection of control and self-efficacy meant horror was displaced by hope.

Our captors took us to a large, abandoned house in the village of Bi'r al 'Ajam – a house hauntingly filled with the remnants of treasured family life covered in the dust of destruction; a house with strong bones that had been shattered by the unrelenting pounding of the war. Pictures of children and proud ancestors leaned precariously into each other, having been turned sideways by explosions.

Covered in dust from the constant shelling were a handcrafted cabinet storing expensive teacups, a table that had undoubtedly hosted rich conversations, treasured carpets and a perfectly crafted silk wall-hanging – all signs of wealth and keepsakes passed down through the generations. This kind of dust did not belong here! Along with every other home in this village, the house had been abandoned in a hurry. All material treasures were left behind. Did they leave voluntarily? Did they leave alive? Either way, the village now bore no resemblance to what it must have been like when the family had lived here.

The night we spent in that abandoned house was no different to any of the other nights we had observed in the months prior. It was a night engulfed in fire and the sounds of blasting. Except now our senses left no room for the impartiality and objectivity expected of a UN military officer. Now, we were inside the fireball of dust, nonsense and distraction we had observed 'objectively' for so long.

For once, we had no chance to report yet another day of pointless devastation. Instead, we were in the epicentre of the artillery and small arms fire. It was all around us instead of below us. We had become soaked in an agonising ordeal, which we had – until now – observed and reported on from a distance.

We were discouraged from speaking to each other. At any given point, we could see at least six others in the room with us, but sometimes more than a dozen armed men would be crowding around us in the holding room. They'd sometimes argue, gesturing to one another, seemingly oblivious to the chaos unfolding around them. With each loud noise and explosion, the three of us braced our bodies involuntarily while the sounds of destruction seemed to wash over our composed captors. The war had become a part of them in a way that seemed inhuman.

At one point, one of our captors approached us. Aggravated, he was pointing at a picture in what looked like his wallet. His family, his children – they were all dead.

After some time debating, discussing and pleading for our lives with them, the oldest of our captors – a dignified man in his seventies – called for our attention. This seemed sudden. In a damaged and dusty Arab–English dictionary, he pointed to the word 'humility' – and that was it. We were free!

Our captivity had ended as abruptly as it had started. Humility had not only prevailed in them, but it had also prevailed in us.

We returned to safety the way we had arrived in the village – by walking across minefields (while quietly humming The Prodigy's 'Mindfields' to lift morale). We walked with our hearts filled with hope, respect, curiosity and love. We returned 'home' having experienced hospitality at the hands of our captors, and we had seen into the lives and minds of those who could have been our tormentors.

There were countless moments in Syria that shaped and framed my study of resilience while also proving that there is no framing human nature. There, we patrolled streets peppered with improvised explosive devices, observed lively, colourful towns turn into spaces of haunting destruction, witnessed children walk calmly to school as crossfire tore their cities apart and sat through nights engulfed in fire and inconceivable suffering. Utter disbelief was then reported objectively and impartially. Occasionally, humility and humanity prevailed.

When we returned to our observation post, we decided we needed to reclaim what had been our home. We wanted to close the loop on the lessons we had learned from our experience. In our sleep-deprived states, those lessons seemed simple, but that was their power.

- Know who you are and sit firmly in your strength.
- Never let fear take you on a walkabout.
- Doubt, fear and the pain of anticipation are no match for hope. You can choose which of them you will keep in your mind.
- When your strength gives in, make things better for others.
- Stay curious and wonder until the last moment.
- Learn from every exposure, even if it seems pointless at the time. You never know when those lessons might come in handy.
- Never stop exploring, even if the distant light of hope seems to be growing dimmer.
- Hold tight to your intent. Engage with your proposition fully.

A year later, I was in the office of Professor Kathryn Pavlovich, who specialises in strategic management, entrepreneurship and sustainability at the University of Waikato. Discussing my experiences, Kathryn effortlessly carried me towards a life-changing epiphany.

'So, what is it that saved you?' she asked. 'Could it have been your curiosity that helped you?' In that instant, the word 'curiosity' gained a new meaning for me.

Choosing to be curious

Many of us only investigate resilience when we feel it is lost. It's only when our resilience reserves are running critically low that we try to find strategies that will help us refill them. To find out more about resilience as a process, it makes sense to explore resilience with people who lean into challenges and to learn from them what it takes to grow resilience deliberately.

We found that whether these resilience heroes sought challenges deliberately or faced challenges they didn't choose, they all displayed high curiosity. Their success was underpinned by the choice to adopt a fundamentally different mindset and to be, as one of them put it, 'a victor rather than a victim.'

Some of the most inspiring people I have ever worked with are Paralympians. One of them shared with me that:

Resilience is about claiming victory over a trial or a setback. Resilience demands you see yourself greater than your trials. You don't define yourself by your setback, but instead by the ways in which you overcame it.

The first step to claiming victory is facing the challenge. There is no better way of building resilience than conditioning an appetite for challenge every minute that you get.

Invariably, this starts with curiosity about us, those around us and the world that lies outside of us. We are all made of the same ingredients when it comes to resilience. It's just that some of us have learned to use the recipe for these ingredients and have tested how the recipe performs in different conditions a little more.

I'd like us to view resilience not as a given or a trait but as a decision or a series of decisions we can make to see ourselves thriving in a way that matters to us. Resilience is not fixed but fluid. It is the immediate and incremental feedback of the decisions we make on what and how to engage, what we envision for ourselves and the world around us, what we choose to sit with and to discard, and most importantly, whether we choose to grow from or reduce ourselves following trials.

Resilience is all about choices. At any junction, we can choose to select or opt out of any opportunity. Unless conditioned to have a resilient mindset, it is likely that we will practise opting out when opportunities are available to us. However, if we can harness our curiosity, our default will become opting in when resilience opportunities arise. Better yet, when curious, we can imagine and create opportunities even when they seem imperceptible.

Every time we make the choice to opt in, to engage with and explore our challenge, we gain confidence that we can at least consider ways to overcome it. We broaden our scope for decision points and the benefits of this confidence may be delivered in the moment, but they also unfold cumulatively over time. By continually deciding to opt in, we create for ourselves evolving, sustained, cumulative resilience. The access point for these decisions lies in curiosity. Curiosity allows us to see challenges as opportunities.

Resilience presents abundant opportunities when we nurture it effectively. It just so happens that conditioning curiosity is the key that unlocks this opportunity.

Psychologist Alexander Watson studied extreme psychological strain during World War I. Watson commented that soldiers whose resilience collapsed under the 'paralysis of the all-powerfulness of war' 'stopped asking questions' and 'ceased to interpret'.

Looking into contemporary warfare, he also reported that 'troops often exhibited curiosity, indicative of an attempt to gather information about their environment and respond to it', and that the maintenance of curiosity about new things was important for sustaining purposeful engagement and, ultimately, for survival. This resounded across all of the environments in which I've researched and worked on resilience – from entrepreneurs and leaders to peak-performing athletes, soldiers and survivors. The ability to wonder and select responses rather than freeze or react in the moment is key for resilience.

We can all thrive if we allow ourselves to continue to ask questions and be curious. Resilience is in the ability to wonder more than worry and to reflect more than ruminate.

For those who thrive in change, ambiguity and unpredictability, curiosity is not just a vehicle for resilience, it is an aim in itself. When you are in a state of curiosity you don't aim to solve as much as understand, fix as much as broaden. Curiosity is an exploration of possibilities, not a seeking of an end.

This sense of curiosity can be a super power that allows us to thrive in ambiguity. It supports our capacity for resilience and underpins the essential mind shift that significant challenges demand from us. Through this mindset, we can engage our capacity to seek and enjoy challenges rather than avoid them, explore opportunities rather than dwell on loss, learn from rather than ruminate on challenging exposures and anticipate positive outcomes rather than only worry about risks.

Curiosity, grounded in self-awareness and fuelled by belonging, aids our ability to reframe challenges, trials and setbacks as valuable opportunities for development. It can even help us develop an appetite for challenges.

As one of our resilience heroes put it: 'Curiosity serves resilience by being the opportunity we give ourselves to be resilient.' He went on to say, 'You give yourself a window of opportunity when you are curious. As an example, in the Special Forces environment, often the only thing you know is that more ambiguity and demands are coming your way if you make it through an obstacle. If you are not curious, you stop just as soon as you see that barrier and hit the wall.'

When I ask any of the mountaineers, entrepreneurs, soldiers, peak-performing athletes and global leaders I've worked with how they developed their capacity for curiosity, they all start their reply with the words, 'I wondered ...'

High achievers like Special Forces operators, Olympic athletes and successful entrepreneurs all come across as if they know what's going to happen next. They all seem to have a sense of calm and composure about them even when they are affected by what is happening to them or around them.

This makes it seem like they have a perfect toolkit to deal with what's occurring, an ability to picture how the situation will unfold, a confidence that they know what sits around every corner and the right skills to tackle whatever it might be.

Imagine my surprise, then, when a seasoned Special Forces soldiers shared with me:

We probably know just enough in these situations. What we know and commit to full-heartedly is the outcome we want to see. If you are curious, you can tackle the unknowns, realign things and piece together the bits of information you have so that you can get across to the other side, without losing your focus on the goal.

If you live life well, you will always find yourself on the spinning edge of possibilities. There, every situation entails elements that are entirely novel – at least to you. So, you have to be ready to evolve and realign, co-create, build new. Curiosity helps you stay engaged in the mission, in your goal, rather than get side-tracked by fear of failure or the threat. It helps you refocus quickly, to focus on results before means.

Curiosity helps us to:

- persevere in pursuit of positive outcomes
- be open to opportunities
- reposition our resources to fit changing demands
- fuel continuous learning
- step into the unknown with greater confidence in our abilities
- recover faster following setbacks.

Curiosity makes us want to explore new things, which can be very rewarding. The thought of potential rewards makes us engage more intentionally with what we're doing, which in turn reduces our risk of feeling helpless, fearful or overwhelmed. Imagine if we could all tune in to the possibility of reward as we navigate more of our trials, be that the reward of becoming a better human, learning more or learning to seek out support.

Curiosity can mean the difference between having focused (on exploring) or narrowed (by fear) attention. An appetite for seeking solutions can also help us overcome mental blocks even in demanding conditions.

Being curious means we're always looking for ways to improve – rather than prove – ourselves. It also helps us to accept and fill gaps in our knowledge and skills, and to distinguish between haphazard and calculated risk. Together, these things result in us having a greater sense of self-belief and trust in our own abilities.

Having a clearer sense of self allows us to be more curious about others. Instead of judging and critiquing them, we find ourselves able to look for common ground or appealing differences. We want to understand them, so that we are able to build relationships and share experiences with them.

When we think of curiosity as a prerequisite for resilience, some of us may be quick to mark ourselves as being low or high on an imaginary continuum. Curiosity is accessible and developable for all of us, and it is something that should be continuously nurtured. All we need to do is get out of curiosity's way more often, and understand and change the ways of thinking, feeling and acting that impede it.

Tool: Curiosity line self-assessment

Place yourself on the curiosity scale.

_____

LOW   **HIGH**

Low = set and safe, fixed and confident in my views, I don't need to change my perspective

High = open to new ideas, willing to change my views, open to change my perspective

What were you considering when you were scoring yourself on that line?

It is difficult to stay curious about all things and all at the same time, and even more so when we are navigating complexity, overwhelming demands or significant challenges. Our curiosity tends to reduce when we feel depleted and pressured. Also we tend to be low on curiosity when we feel we have fixed views on people or events around us.

How we engage with change and ambiguity may drive growth and development, or territoriality, desire to prove rather than improve ourselves, or do better than someone else rather than doing better than we did yesterday. Ask yourself:

- Whether high or low, what were the references you used to assess yourself that way?
- Looking into the way you live your life and engage with your environment, how curious are you?
- What are you curious about?
- What are you not curious about?
- If you're not curious, what views, ideas, obstacles prevent you from being so?
- How does your curiosity serve you?
- How does your curiosity deplete you?
- How might curiosity serve you better?

Curiosity – the secret sauce of resilience

When I started researching resilience, I saw curiosity as the premise of fictional characters the likes of Peter Pan and Jack Sparrow – mischief mixed with muse, frivolity and the mystical. As a result, I felt awkward asking members of the SAS about it.

When interviewing Soldier R, I hesitantly asked, 'Do you think curiosity might support your resilience?'

He laughed and said, 'Do you mean like Pippi Longstocking? Of course! Curiosity is key for resilience. Every opportunity we grant ourselves to be resilient demands a degree of curiosity. Every single one of them.'

He then went on to describe his colleagues: 'However different we may be, we are all "bright eyes and bushy tail" type people. What separates us from the rest is our ability to think outside the square, to ask questions. To be resilient, you must be ready to adapt and to invent better ways of doing things, better ways of being, always. It is about asking the "What if?" question at times when there seems to be little or no way out.

'If we have any superpowers, they stem from curiosity. An example is right here on my badge.' He pointed to his sand-coloured beret.

'Embroidered on it is "Who Dares Wins". Curiosity is the backbone to it. We are curiosity.'

As my research deepened, it became apparent that curiosity was something elite soldiers had conditioned deliberately and diligently into themselves as a matter of survival. It was an essential prerequisite for their success, not just a frivolous preference. As a result, they were ready to be challenged, to challenge and to commit to learning.

Another soldier responded by saying: 'Sometimes, it can be as simple as just wanting to find out what it will be like to take another step toward your goal – and for that, you need to espouse curiosity and forsake fear.'

When curiosity becomes a practised and rehearsed part of our way of being, it allows us a moment to pause before responding to the changes, triggers and events around us, a moment in time to interrupt those negative predictions that we make out of habit, may it be pessimistic or habitual.

9. Curiosity and possibilities

Soldier Y

'Curiosity is asking questions with a purpose. If there is to be a challenge in life, curiosity helps you deliver your best response.' These are the words of Soldier Y, who shared with me the story of one of the most testing moments of his life.

The insurgents show no regard to whether their assault will impact combatants, that six-year-old chasing joy with a dusty ball down the street or his anxious mother moving through the market. Her hope that today she can afford to break the dry-bread diet for what is left of her family is of no relevance to the insurgents.

Dusk sets. So does the enemy's intent – to control and to terrorise. Their fire lands in the civilian area, tormenting everyone who runs for safety, by scattering and spraying bullets like a heavy summer rain.

The small military team rapidly deployed to help cease the torment is already on site. The source of fire is quickly located through the erratic movements that he makes. Suddenly, the seconds grow long as Soldier X, charged with apprehending the insurgent, collapses to the ground.

Rushing to his friend's aid, Soldier Y – a highly trained combat medic – hears the final rapid breaths of his friend. Just hours earlier, Y had been hearing the same rapid breaths from X, but then it was because he'd been laughing at his own outlandish ideas for life after his deployment, while trying to keep a cup of instant coffee from spilling all over the table. The time for those outlandish ideas will never come for X now.

Y knows there is no helping X – these breaths are just his body's final reaction to the shock. Soldier Y's best friend's life was taken not by erratic fire, but by a precise shot to the head. In those same long seconds, Soldier Y sees his best friend's killer.

The killer is also wounded, but alive and in pain. Y rushes to the killer's aid – he has now become Y's patient. It is not Y's role to place judgement; it is his role to help a fellow human.

As Y is strapping the wounds of yet another victim of war, he recognises the similarities between his best friend and his patient. He too is someone's son, perhaps a parent, a neighbour and a fellow human tormented by the war.

The pain was still there for Y, but he was able to choose his actions. His purpose was, first and foremost, to save lives. Wrapped around this purpose was the acceptance that he was not to judge one life as more worthy than another.

As a soldier, he also had to have faith that the vehicles for justice exist and that he would be able to help demonstrate how they work through his actions. He knew that if he was to react in rage, he too would become a part of the narrative of hatred. He wanted his patient to live and understand that a system of justice and process existed. He wanted his patient's life to continue as an example of humanity extended to someone who wasn't able to display it himself.

If this was to create even a moment of doubt in the next terrorist charging forward to take a soldier's life or the lives of innocent civilians, then that moment, that second of doubt had the potential to save the lives of many.

Soldier Y was able to take these heroic actions because he was clear and grounded in his purpose long before the incident took place. The way he engaged with this scenario was because he was clear on it. His purpose did not emerge from his actions. His actions emerged from his purpose. He did not react to a situation. He engaged with it.

Soldier Y did get overtaken by grief over the loss of his friend. Every August, he thinks about where his friend would be right now if he hadn't been killed. He thinks of his friend so intensely and vividly that he feels he is building a parallel life for him. Wondering what he would be doing right now has allowed Soldier Y to build an entire world of possibilities.

Soldier Y would argue that his resilience was strengthened because of the way he engaged in this incident. He had an opportunity to test his values and purpose in that moment, and he has since evolved and deepened them. After leaving the unit, he served internationally with the UN and other not-for-profit organisations. He has helped build businesses and communities, and most importantly, he has deepened his appreciation for how purpose strengthens resilience.

Curiosity helped him manage this situation, but it wasn't something he stumbled upon accidentally in that moment. The moment was merely a demonstration of the benefits of the curiosity he had developed in the lead-up to the event, in the knowledge that curiosity was vital for resilience. Y would say, 'Curiosity helps you create options and gain access to that crucial measure of self and situational awareness – the knowledge of "when to be what". It affords the freedom to make room for and amplify your vision, even when it seems your fate is sealed, or when poor choices, or reactions from habit may seem justified.'

Soldier Y's response shows us that there is always something we can do to improve our situation. The predicament is just a starting point; an invitation to grow if we are curious, the start of a downward spiral if we are not.

Resilience is not a reaction

Some situations demand nothing more than a reaction. If you accidentally touch something hot, you only need to pull away from the heat. If you see your child heading towards an incoming vehicle, you only need to yank them out of harm's way. These are simple scenarios for which we are geared to respond. The options are black and white – stay and get hurt or move and reduce the risk of further pain. These black-and-white scenarios are not tests for resilience.

It takes more than reactions to reach resilience. To be resilient, we need to accept that our brains may read many situations as if they involve hot objects or oncoming vehicles. However, resilience is not a reaction. It is a process underpinned by decision points. Sometimes, it will involve a single, critical decision point flashing in bright lights right before our eyes, but more often, it will feature a series of tiny, incremental, pivotal decision points, each of which contributes towards a markedly better script for our lives.

When we stop being curious we begin to view challenges as closed-off loops of finite options and limited, fixed solutions. Practising curiosity, even if it is in how we might respond more optimally to the challenges around us, can be invaluable.

After some repetition, these decision points can create solid platforms, stepping stones formed by deeper awareness, confidence and skillsets. These can be lifesaving, especially when change, ambiguity and unpredictability leave us feeling like we are spinning out of control. From these platforms, we can springboard into our next opportunity for thriving.

If we play it right, we can rehearse our resilience moves to the point where we can recognise that an opportunity for promotion, a setback, a toxic relationship, a grumpy boss, a self-destructive pattern or a complex task provide us with opportunities to observe, lean into, explore, learn and pivot. They are not hot objects or incoming vehicles.

One Special Forces operator put it like this: 'Fear braces us tight at first and then makes us soft around the edges. We learn to stay put, frozen, pre-empting and living the worst-case scenario, long before it was even a possibility.'

Resilience becomes an opportunity when the challenge of moving seems greater than the option of staying put. Unless it is a hot object we have landed on, movement always presents as a greater challenge than staying put. We are designed to avoid strain, doubly so when it may not guarantee positive outcomes. We also avoid strain when our desired outcome may seem out of reach. We are cued to settle for the familiar, even if it is not what's best for us. The trouble is our growth, healing and thriving are always preceded by strain.

Resilience is also possible when we feel like we have reached a finite conclusion, when it seems we've hit the end of the road, or when the road ahead seems to be blocked. In these cases, we often choose to just stand there and handle the despair. However, resilience isn't in enduring strain – that's just grit!

Resilience is in slowing time and shifting our perspective enough to see how we can secure the load more effectively, to see what we feel as a burden transform into a platform for us to stand on, to look around that obstacle long enough and notice that beyond it might lie abundant potential. A change of perspective can show us that the boulder in our way can become a stepping stone towards an endless field of opportunities.

Remember, although your brain likes the familiar, it thrives on the road less travelled. Resilience is a possibility we need to afford ourselves more often, and this is where the crucial element of curiosity kicks in.

In her TED talk, Canadian neuroscientist Lisa Feldman Barrett says: 'We think we are hardwired for certain emotions, but we are not. You can have more control over your emotions than you think you do. It may feel to you like your emotions are hardwired and they just trigger and happen to you, but they don't.

'Emotions are guesses that your brain constructs in the moment, where billions of brain cells are working together. You have more control over those guesses than you might imagine. Your predictions are basically the way your brain works – it's business as usual. Your predictions are the basis of every experience that you have. They are the basis of every action that you take. Predictions are primal. They help us to make sense of the world in a quick and efficient way.'

Lisa's suggestion is that we can learn to see and experience things differently by learning to construct our emotions differently. We can go from prediction to determination and energise our brains to predict a different outcome. In the context of stress, anxiety and emotional suffering, Lisa calls this 'getting your butterflies to fly in formation'.

Lisa goes on to say, 'Emotions that seemed to happen to you are made by you. Your brain is wired so that if you change, the ingredients that your brain uses to make emotion can transform your life. I am telling you that you have the capacity to turn down the dial on emotional suffering and its consequences for your life by learning how to construct your experiences differently.'

By tapping into curiosity, the temptation to dive into a fight/flight/freeze response is reduced and replaced with a sense of calm, an ability to select one's state of mind and being and to shape the outcomes of our encounters in a way that is congruent with our best vision of ourselves. We get there by leaning into the resilience opportunity.

10. Things that matter take effort

Janet

As a psychologist, I have had the opportunity to work alongside some of the most remarkable practitioners in the field – one of them is Janet.

Janet trained as a clinical psychologist in Europe, then worked in Australia before returning to her home country of South Africa. She would call herself 'old school', but she was always 10 steps ahead of the rest when it came to anything new or cutting edge. She was also well known for keeping other practitioners in check by really testing the extent to which they knew what their best was and whether they were able to will themselves to sustain their best. Janet did not tolerate 'meeker practitioners' – people who had the status, training and influence to act but, as she'd put it, who would 'dilly dally on the peripheries and in indecision'.

Her practice was uncompromising – the product of decades of the most carefully curated techniques, deep research, compassion, empathy and dedication to healing generational trauma. She was deeply committed to the causes she served, and she had no tolerance for racism, sexism, ageism or anything that subtracted the capacity for individuals and communities to thrive. She made it her mission to combat any obstructions or limitations to that capacity in the most impactful way she knew – by healing, strengthening and liberating survivors.

Janet was frighteningly straight up with the truth she observed. Yet somehow, she delivered her wisdom in a way that made you feel safe and cared for.

Janet was in her final months of life having battled cancer for years when I got to work with her at a practitioners' retreat. There, her focus was as much on our case studies as it was on those of us who brought them to light. Her tempo was unrelenting and hard to keep up with, but her passion was contagious. You just had to stay with her.

We had been asked to come to the retreat having identified one challenge that, if we could overcome it, would make an exponential difference in our lives. We also needed to have identified why that shift might be difficult for us.

Janet appeared to be listening attentively as we introduced ourselves and told our stories. Once we had concluded our stories, she delivered her welcome speech. Polite as her delivery was, her message was confronting: 'My job is to sit with you at this bus stop and see you get on your tomorrow bus. Frankly, all you seem to care about is finding the next person who will listen to your reasons for staying fixed at your current locations, and that isn't going to be me for long.

'Are you heading some place, or will you sit around trying to convince me you have had it hard? I can't fathom how you are able to stand up with this chunky sequence of defeatist stories in your heads. You won't fit through the bus door if you keep clutching on to these concrete blocks you have borrowed as interpretations for your random sources of self-constructed misery.

'I gotta tell you, by the time you've each walked me to your present moments, I am bored and exhausted – and I am only here listening to you. The stories you tell yourselves are so fixed I can signpost every junction of your narratives with ease, if it wasn't that your labels were ably borrowed from others.

'I don't care about what has happened. Things happen, people happen when they choose their lessons learned. I care about what you have learned, how you have turned these learnings into fuel, and your knowledge of what else you need to scoop up on the way to tomorrow. That's it! So, are you heading some place next, what will you chose to take and how will you make this move a no brainer?'

Janet's wisdom was easily accessible. It was what we all knew we needed to think like, feel like, act like – but, at the start of that retreat, we all knew we were lacking in some way. We were issuing out the perceived challenge and indulging in perceived causes behind the strain we felt, stopping ourselves from shifting to a better place in our lives and work. What we were missing was the conviction, imagination and curiosity to explore alternatives, which made it impossible for us to shift to better.

Janet then added: 'Now I'm going to give you a break. I'll congratulate you. Just by knowing and feeling there is better, you are calculating, exploring, discovering alternatives. Fearfully, by the sounds of things, but evidently you are and that's the best part. You have also likely observed, imagined or accumulated enough to know that there may be a starting point in the direction of travel.'

Difficult things matter

There is a saying that goes, 'Never get on a train without knowing exactly where the tracks lead.' It has a merit when you translate it to the context of purpose. More of us are paralysed by indecision than by bad decisions. Indecision is what leads many of us to make bad decisions.

The fact that you are aware of the need for better means that you are capable of better. Let me say it again: the fact that you are aware of the need for better means that you are capable of better.

There isn't a parallel universe you need to make a quantum leap to get to 'better'. Things that matter, the hard things, have always taken effort. If something is difficult, that's just a sign that it matters for building resilience.

The big question is why is it so hard to take consistent actions in the direction of what's better? Because it takes effort to shift the status quo. To do this, you need to use your imagination to envisage what that better state looks like. The more you do this, the more your current state will feel intolerable.

If you want to make a shift but it feels difficult, consistency and curiosity are what will help you move away from the status quo.

The biggest pain we cause ourselves is in knowing we can be better, knowing enough to locate ourselves in our present moment and choosing not to take action because we think it's supposed to be easy.

All you need is direction of travel. The rest will follow when you start, so look towards where you're heading, start travelling and don't stop unless you are unable to adjust your bearings on the go. As Janet would say: 'Now you know better, do better.' Often what is on the way of us doing better when we know better is procrastination. There is a trick to unlocking potential there, too.

Procrastination

Procrastination amplifies the gap between where you are and where you think you ought to be. Is this something you will fix today? No? OK, if you can't break your pattern of behaviour then change your relationship with it by understanding the purpose it serves – to keep your brain from burning down. The most sustainable way to commit is to change your relationship with procrastination.

Tool: Write your procrastination story

Write your story of procrastination. Describe what you avoid and how you avoid it. Try to suspend all judgement and simply describe your behavior as if you are an impartial observer.

- *Write about your procrastination as if it was a wondrous little quirk and not the horrendous curse you think it is.*
- *Be very careful and respectful here. What is the need that this behaviour meets? Reflect and explore what your procrastination is aiming to protect you from.*

What is the need to be met? To change and outgrow the habit of procrastination, your body and brain want to be interested, to be calm, to be confident. What better ways do you have of doing this? Do them daily and be mindful of the need that you are meeting. If you fall off the procrastination-loving wagon, see that need. Did it morph?

Is your procrastination an easily accessible thing you have practised to perfection while trying to fulfil another need that you are too busy to notice? What might that need be? Listen to yourself. 'I am so tired. I don't even want to think about doing this but I have to, so I will sit myself on this chair and stare at the screen in the hope that something meaningful happens.'

Procrastination is sometimes a signal that you are brutal on yourself.

Instead of sitting there staring at your screen, try pausing for a moment to work out what it is you actually want or need. Expand your options.

If you were starving and all you had in front of you was a bag of chips, would you eat them? Of course. But if you stopped for a moment and thought about what would sustain and nourish you – and you knew that very meal was in your kitchen, would you still eat the chips?

The same goes for procrastination. Take a moment and think about what options are in front of you that will help you to be at your best. Is your aim to sit there or to be creative? If you are tired, rest.

Rewriting your narrative

R

R works in emergency services and is ex-military. His wife and child were killed in a car accident more than 10 years ago. He blames himself and those around him. His life has become a dreary wasteland of chronic guilt, anger and judgement. He's moved away from his religious faith and, by doing so, removed himself from his community.

'I lost my child and wife in a car accident. I am still devastated, even though I lost them a decade ago. The guilt continues to eat away at me. The minute I stop keeping busy, it takes over like a thick, dark fog ... I do whatever it takes to cope.

'I'd see other families with children around me and I'd be overtaken by envy and anger. If they only knew what they had! I'd give anything to be like them.

'For years the grief and guilt would drive me to self-destructive behaviours – drinking excessively, picking fights, avoiding conversations and any interventions from friends and family that aimed to shift me to a better place. I isolated myself and ran away from any possibility of developing intimate relationships with others. I closed my world right down to the bare minimum.'

Replay? Rewrite!

In order to change the narratives we live with we need to accept what has happened.

Acceptance means taking a note of where an event has ended then deliberately choosing what lessons to move forward with. Those lessons are not always readily available at the finish line of that event. They morph and shift with us often in a way that seems outside of our control. Some of us try to avoid thinking about these events, but more often, we replay them and reminisce about them.

We need to ask ourselves what we learned from these events. If we are to stand with resilience, we have to locate our best stance yet and be prepared to regain that stance every time our new experiences push us off balance.

It is never a single epiphany that takes us onto the next platform of happiness and purpose. There will always be trip-ups. Our brains, our lives and our memories run on a repeat reel if we let them.

For R, the process of rewriting his narrative looks like this:

I lost my wife and child in a car accident.

From	To
I am still devastated, even though I lost them a decade ago.	Over the decade, I worked on transforming the devastation into a feeling of deep gratitude and appreciation that I was once loved and I loved so deeply.
The guilt continues to eat away at me.	I learned that the guilt I used to feel was my way of trying to control what had already happened. I accepted I could not change what has happened. I developed instead a deep appreciation for life – its richness, abundance and complexities. I have replaced that need to control with commitment to positively influence everything that comes my way.
The minute I stop keeping busy it takes over like a thick, dark fog ... I do whatever it takes to cope.	The sadness will always be there. Rather than avoiding it, when I feel it coming, I make the space to sit with it and cherish the memories of my loved ones.

From	To
I'd see other families with children around me and be overtaken by envy and anger. If they only knew what they had! I'd give anything to be like them.	I've built the strength to see the beauty in others and appreciate the magic of life and love, rather than envy others. Now, when I see happy families, I feel a part of this gift. I have had this gift. I am so grateful to have felt it and I am filled with joy when I notice it around me.
For years the grief and guilt would drive me to self-destructive behaviours – drinking excessively, picking fights, avoiding conversations and interventions from friends and family that aimed to shift me to a better place.	When others check in on me and try to help me, even if their attempts seem naive, I pause and let gratitude take over. I am worthy of care and love. I know this healing matters to them as much as me. I respond in kind with love and care back and that fuels me. By letting them help me I strengthen those around me.
I isolated myself, running away from any possibility of developing intimate relationships with others. I closed my world right down to the bare minimum.	My greatest pivot was letting the walls around me fall. I accepted I have nothing to hide from. I opened my world and, with that, I learned that many others have felt what I felt, so I have grown to bring light and hope for others.

<u>Vienna</u>

Vienna has had a string of bad relationships, one after another. She often finds herself replaying conversations in her mind long after they happened. 'Then he said and then I said and then you said …' All that is going on is the confirmation that things are not the way they ought to be. She thought there was a reliable recipe that would make things turn out just right if she followed its exact measurements and steps.

'My fiancé broke up with me three years ago. Initially I barged on in, trying to maintain whatever "status" and level of life I had constructed for myself. The ripple effects of this break-up and the betrayal it involved spilled across every aspect of my life. I was going to be the big earner in this relationship. I poured my heart and soul into carving out a successful career so we could afford all we wanted in life.

'We purchased our first home, and I was so proud to be able to fully cover the deposit. I had the kids planned. In the next ten years there was going to be a holiday home and I knew I'd be a partner in the firm by then, so I'd scheduled in my head the holiday destinations we were going to travel to.

'After the break-up I had to sell the house. Then I rushed into a tonne of dates, trying to find someone who would fit my life plan. What else did I have to live for? My biological clock was ticking.

'Then I began to hate and blame my career for the loss of my relationship. I couldn't blame Kane anymore, so I started underperforming and lost my ranking at work. Then I blamed my upbringing and my overambitious parents, who made me think that I was only worthy if I achieved.'

Suddenly, Vienna came to the realisation that there were no faults and blames left for her to go after anymore. She realised she was stuck in despair. She was clutching on to any evidence that the collapse of her perfect life plan was not her fault. She shared: 'I realised, at one point, I can go on and blame anything – the politics in the US, the pandemic, social media or the climate crisis. It didn't matter what I imagined I could blame. None of this changed where I was in my life right now.'

My fiancé broke up with me three years ago.

From	To
Initially I barged on in trying to maintain whatever 'status' and level of life I had constructed for myself.	I accepted that it was OK for me to let the grief take over long enough for me to process the loss. I am allowed to grieve a vision I had created for myself. I needed to let myself say goodbye to the vision I had crafted. This allowed me to accept that losing that version of me was not going to define my happiness or my purpose! It was just one version. I am worth it just as I am now, no matter what transpires – not because of what happens next or what has been, but because of exactly who I am now in this very moment, bruises and all.

From	To
The ripple effects of this break-up and the betrayal it involved have spilled across every aspect of my life. I was going to be the big earner in this relationship. I poured my heart and soul into carving a successful career so we could afford all that we wanted in life. We purchased our first home, and I was so proud to be able to fully cover the deposit.	I paused to appreciate my strengths, my capabilities, my grit. I paused to acknowledge I was capable of supporting myself and others. I appreciated my generosity and the strength of my will. I also appreciated that I don't need to carry the world's responsibilities on my shoulders. I deserve to be cared for as much as I am willing to care for others.
I had the kids planned and scheduled. In the next 10 years there was going to be the holiday home, and I knew I'd be a partner by then so could schedule in my head the locations we were going to travel to. After the break-up, I had to sell the house. I rushed into a tonne of dates, trying to find someone who would fit my life plan. What else did I have to live for? My biological clock was ticking.	I was grateful to have developed such strong family values. My desire to have children remained but I discovered there are countless way in which I could invest my resources and share my love, even if I never had children of my own. Importantly, I was not going to chase for someone to fit a timeline. I wasn't going to rush this because I learned, for once, to really enjoy my own company.

From	To
I began to hate and blame my career for the loss of the relationship. I couldn't blame Kane anymore, so I started underperforming and lost my ranking at work.	I gained so much humility following the loss of my job. The world was no longer divided into successful and unsuccessful humans. We were all humans navigating the complexities of life. When I opened up, I discovered my experiences are by no means unique. We all struggle and trip up sometimes. We just have to learn from these moments.
I blamed my upbringing and my overambitious parents, who made me think I was worthy of what I achieved.	I paused to appreciate how loved I was by my parents. They came from a different time in history. They wanted me to be as resilient and capable as I could be, so I can stand on my own two feet and experience the best of life. I also realised I no longer needed to pursue their approval. I could craft and follow my own rules. As a result, my relationship with them deepened.

Tool: Start with it!

Consider some of the depleting narratives you have accumulated or are holding onto in your life. How might you rewrite these narratives for yourself, as R and Vienna did?

Lean into this exercise by challenging your perspective. Engage with it differently to achieve a different result. Begin to explore these as possibilities. You don't have to commit to a different way of thinking, acting or feeling, but simply explore alternatives. Remember, the more you realise that those alternatives exist and that you are capable of dreaming them up, the more you fuel and sustain your resilience.

Exploring alternative ways of thinking, feeling and acting is key to resilience when we feel stuck. Not all alternatives will stick and it is important that we are prepared that some may offer only a temporary respite from the all too familiar despair or burden of the past or worry for the future. What matters is that the alternative is becoming stuck, and that we commit to conjure alternatives and explore them, rather than enduring the pain of yesterday without giving any chance for the light to shine on the opportunity of today.

11. Be ready to learn

Crucible moments

Crucible moments are defining moments in our lives. They are transformative experiences because they cause us to shift the ways we think, feel and act. The shifts we experience change us. They alter our identity. This new form of identity can be better or worse than when the defining moment found us. To pivot to better we need curiosity.

Every example of remarkable resilience I have come across involves a version of extraordinary feats of resilience. Everyone I studied demonstrated that their resilience was fundamentally about their ability to observe, select and influence their thoughts, feelings and actions. They had all stumbled upon gold dust – the realisation that when under significant pressure our most readily available responses are often negatively laden ones.

According to Dr David Dawkins, 'On an average day, uninterrupted, 80 per cent of our thoughts are negative, 70–80 per cent are repeated daily.' Research published by the National Science Foundation in 2015 upped the ante, saying that 95 per cent of our thoughts are repetitive. If the average person has between 12,000 and 60,000 thoughts a day, that's a lot of negative chatter.

If that's an average day, imagine what happens when we are confronted by the overwhelming, challenging and unexpected. The good news is that this repetitive negativity is not a sign of us being negative or pessimistic. It simply illustrates that our busy minds are wired to protect us, calculating risks around every corner. Our lives have become infinitely more complex and intricate. However, the tiny part of our brain responsible for detecting threat, the amygdala, is still wired to escalate perceptions of risk as if a wild bear was trying to get us. While punching (fight), fleeing (flight) or playing dead (freeze) when we're upset with our boss may not be a proportionate reaction to a deadline, we are still wired to react.

People who grow through crucible moments have learned that, no matter their circumstances, the states they experience are temporary, unconscious and when left unchecked, often sub-optimal. They have learned to observe these states without allowing them to become all-engulfing and they have recalibrated the ways in which they felt and thought so that their actions were more aligned with their aim. They have learned to observe their thoughts and emotions, and they found the power to select how to construct their lives the way they wanted, by choosing the ways in which they felt, thought and acted. The key to this selection process is to *interrupt* the habitual patterns of thought and select optimal ones instead.

Don't be afraid to fail

When you let curiosity in, it shelters you from fight/flight/
freeze mode long enough to see past the obstacles you
encounter. You can only be one or the other: you can either
choose to stay with negative emotions, or you can choose to
switch your whole brain on and consciously choose 'better'.
If you choose to be curious, you'll end up with many more
options to work with.

When we choose to wonder more, rather than allow ourselves
to lock into reactions or habitual responses, curiosity has the
capacity to turn fear, anxiety, pain and grief into purposeful,
positive action. Curiosity can:

- turn woe to wonder
- make the impossible plausible
- turn unsettling into exciting
- help you seek rather than avoid challenges.

Being curious makes finding a way to work through challenges
a whole lot more rewarding. Challenges then become
surmountable; the unknown ceases to overwhelm, it 'just is',
and we learn there is no sense being fearful or anxious about
setbacks or challenges.

In every experience, there are gains to be made through
learning. When tested, it is defeatist and sometimes even fatal
if you don't try to improve your situation. Being prepared

to fail is the price you pay when you commit to pursuing something better.

The most consistent advice from everyone I have studied is, 'You should not be afraid to fail.' If you focus more on what you could gain and on being neutral about failure, then you allow yourself to be more focused on generating possibilities for success, learning and discovery even when you feel most tested.

If you nurture your curiosity-in-action, even when you fail, curiosity will help you pick yourself back up again, so you can continue to learn. Instead of quitting or, worse, not even trying, through curiosity, you will keep striving for solutions. It will help you shift from 'I'm in trouble here' mode to thinking 'I can tackle this'.

Curiosity plays a critical role in controlling negative emotions in challenging times. By harnessing it, we can negate the effects of fear that might otherwise limit our capacity to explore ideas. Fear is never a solution to anything. It is just an indication that there is something in there that matters to you and a signal that you must get yourself into a focused, thinking, doing mode.

Curiosity tilts us towards success in situations we may otherwise view as unresolvable. Even when we feel we are nearing a breaking point, curiosity can help us to recover, to accept that breaking point is just a state of mind and to believe that we never truly reach our full potential. As a mindset, curiosity reminds us that life can be a worthy adventure, if we let it. We fail the minute we stop seeking to be challenged and be better.

If you are not curious, you will give up at the first obstacle. To survive and thrive, we need to allow ourselves the space to be surprised, to discover and to adapt. After all, uncertainty is our only certainty.

Negative emotions travel together. They have a way of amplifying their presence and importance to us, of nudging their way into our conscious and subconscious. Fear feeds on fear and feeds fear. Hesitance does the same. Like resilience, these are practised attitudes that shape every aspect of our lives.

Mind the grit in your shoe

Often the biggest drains on our resilience don't emerge as a consequence of crucible moments or acute events. Instead, they come as a result of lots of tiny, depleting thoughts, feelings or experiences, which cumulatively amount to heavy loads.

I was once told: 'Mind the tiny grit in your shoe, as it can be your ultimate undoing.'

Once you recognise that the issues you are avoiding to confront have turned into 'grit in your shoe', try to work out why you've let them build up. Pause to appreciate what you stand to lose and what do you stand to gain by confronting those issues.

These pieces of grit may include your attitudes towards the people in your life you tolerate but struggle to fully accept or understand, unaddressed resentment towards others in your past, regret or perceived failure points you try to mask.

Elizabeth, the high achiever I described in chapter five, explained how she dealt with the resentment towards her mother and her childhood experiences. She realised that what was depleting her resilience the most was not her memories of childhood, but the shame she felt about holding so much resentment about her past. Her solution was simple but liberating:

Rather than judging myself for being judgey, I chose to tap into empathy, compassion and most importantly – curiosity towards myself and others.

By tapping into curiosity about herself and others, rather than trying to prove herself right or worthy, she realised everyone could hold the opinions that feel true to them. Those opinions didn't have to define her or her experience of life. Elizabeth added: 'I made myself an imaginary T-shirt with the slogan: "What other people think of me is none of my business." There is no arrogance to this statement. It holds the realisation that it is unbecoming for me to think that people spend so much time focusing on me. It was also a reminder that I have more meaningful things to do than worry about people's opinions. I wear this imaginary T-shirt every day.'

Her hurtful past was no longer a tiny piece of grit in her shoe that she needed to endure. Instead, she focused on exploring why 'hurt people hurt people.' In her words: 'What might have hurt that person to the point that it's made them want to cause harm to others?'

There is a lesson to be gained in adopting Elizabeth's approach. By employing curiosity, we can better respond to and engage with interpersonal differences, de-escalate conflict and minimise the risk of us picking up a piece of grit to carry in our shoe. We sometimes fail to appreciate that there are powerful undercurrents that affect how people view and engage with the world. Often, these are unconsciously held values, beliefs and assumptions, patterns we have inherited from our upbringing and personality traits we seldom understand. Rather than reacting or absorbing, we can practise observing and exploring.

Often, the differences we come across or the experiences that jolt us unexpectedly are a matter of disrupted expectations. We all run on our own unique script for life, but sometimes different scripts collide. By employing curiosity, we invite possibilities that challenge our assumptions and expectations, inviting us to grow. Like Elizabeth, we can choose to wonder more than worry, by asking exploratory questions such as:

- What different lessons have others come across?
- What opportunity may become available to me if I learn to be more gracious in the way I engage with others?

- What is the fear that is holding me/others hostage and restricting understanding?
- What might be others'/my unmet needs?

The white noise of gossip

Have you ever stopped to notice the waves of sound when you're in a cafe away from the beach? It is a 'h-sh-h-sh-i-s-h-i-h' like sound, and it's loudest when there are several small groups of two or three to a table. I challenge you to listen out for it because what you're hearing is the sound of gossip. I first realised this when I worked in cafes and restaurants as a university student.

'H-sh-h-sh-i-s-hi-h' translates to 'He said and then she said and then I said and then he said ...' and so on. As you listen, it may seem that the event you are hearing about has happened in the past, but it is actually happening in the mind of the storyteller as they tell the story, and it will pivot, sway and change depending on the reaction of the listeners. It is like a choose your own adventure book being written right before your eyes. These waves of gossip happen at most tables, albeit with slightly different themes depending on who is creating them.

When I first started noticing this, I assumed it was a cultural thing – that people in the West were more inclined to speak about others than about themselves. It dawned on me it was not about East vs West. People the world over gossip. It is just that the sound of gossip in English was new to me. Then I began to wonder what connected these people. I wondered if they ever spoke about what went on within themselves.

Why do they talk about others? Is this their way of belonging, bonding and understanding themselves better?

Through gossiping with others or as part of our internal monologue, we let other people live rent free in our minds a lot more than we can afford. We are sense-making in all the wrong ways.

Gossip isolates us. It polarises and separates us from others, from learning and from growth. It has a limiting aim that sounds like this: 'I am right, they are wrong'; 'I am good, they are not'; 'I am better, they are worse'; 'I am in, they are out.'

Resilient people are more interested in learning from differences than judging them. They seek to understand rather than prove, to connect rather than separate. Curiosity sustained SAS members' ability to respect and relate to others, benevolently and empathetically. In the words of one SAS member: 'To look past a pile of differences takes curiosity. Through curiosity, you can overcome your biases and even ill feelings. The amount of curiosity you can summon informs the way you orient yourself and deal with different people and ultimately shapes your outcome in the moment and beyond.'

Curiosity was of critical importance to the ability of Special Forces operators to adapt to their context and to 'really understand those around them'. This was particularly important when 'fear and ambiguity can drive polarising views'.

Another person I spoke to explained this further by adding that success and survival in the SAS 'is not only a matter of looking out for and being respectful of differences but also really asking yourself why those differences exist. It demands that you study the undercurrents that shape the space you are in mindfully and with respect.'

He also said that curiosity guided him in finding a 'genuine and common ground' with people of other cultures and aided him in de-escalating potentially lethal situations.

Why does exploring a topic like gossip matter for resilience? Because resilience is about being able to manage where your attention goes and how you invest your energy. Gossip can be a little like rumination – a closed loop that reinforces an often self-indulgent narrative.

You power your resilience by broadening your understanding. The fundamental rule for resilience is to move lightly on your feet and in your mind.

Instead of gossiping

Carrying curiosity, compassion and empathy is a whole lot lighter then carrying judgement. Choose to wonder. Choose to challenge yourself.

Commit to this especially when you think your view of someone is pretty much fixed. In some extreme circumstances, it might not change your relationship with them, but it will improve your relationship with yourself further.

If you want to be resilient, you'll learn quickly that there is only so far you can go in your own mind before you have to explore the mind of another.

Growth versus fixed mindset

When asked what motivated him to pursue a career with a team, an SAS soldier said: 'So I know that after I accomplish each challenge there will be no delay before I can ask myself "OK, what next?" and know that it'll be just as good as the last challenge.'

This is an example of a crucial resilience characteristic we all need to practise more – the growth mindset. Something resilient people display in abundance. They've learned to seek and enjoy challenges rather than avoid them. They've trained themselves to view challenges as surmountable. They accept change and ambiguity as the norm.

Dr Carol Dweck is an American psychologist who has spent her career focusing on motivation and mindset. Dr Dweck has condensed decades of research into this powerful message: our successes or failures are less about our innate abilities or intellect, but instead about whether we approach our challenges with a growth or a fixed mindset.

Fixed mindset	Growth mindset
I want to prove myself	I want to improve myself
I seek to be better than others	I seek to be better than I was yesterday
I avoid challenges and being challenged	I seek challenges, they are opportunities
I avoid hard things	I do hard things/I persevere when things are hard
My skills and capabilities are predetermined	I can develop my skills and capabilities
No point trying if I fail	If I fail, I learn and try again
I seek only positive feedback	I seek all feedback, so I can grow
I am threatened by other people's successes	I am inspired by other people's successes
I avoid self-reflection	I reflect on myself
I seek people who think just like me	I am open to different views and ideas

When I asked about the importance of a growth mindset, one person I interviewed said: 'Readiness and appetite for cumulative growth through challenges is essential for survival and success. True challenges and trials are seldom predictable or about the known. If you don't step outside your comfort zone, you will never know what you could do or experience. The question "What would it be like if …?" is a question we always have at the back of our minds when we approach challenges, and this is fundamentally a question of curiosity.'

From choosing to persevere through pain and strain through to finding the capacity to envision and work through out-of-the-box solutions, unless we are curious, finding a way to work through the challenges that get handed to us can become the heaviest drag.

I started asking what some of the most resilient people do to manage the burdens of continuous change, ambiguity and unpredictability in their lives. In a typical fashion they made it sound simple: shift or drop. Here is how one of the resilience heroes described it:

> Things are not what they are, they are what you make them be. Resilience gives in along the way when we carry unnecessary load. You cannot expect yourself to perform well, to survive and thrive, if you are carrying endless dusty folders of unattended, depleting or irrelevant content.

> You have to learn the discipline to drop what you cannot change or what depletes you, or – when you cannot drop it – to shift your mindset so that you start seeing it as something that fuels you, or at least as something that doesn't detract from you.

The idea of reducing worries and broadening resilience by using a simple 'shift or drop' inventory seems endlessly appealing.

Training yourself to access your best

The military trains the capacity to endure and operate effectively in significant challenges. Service personnel go through phases and stages of training that teach them to strip away the white noise in their minds and commit to perseverance, adaptation, focus and endurance. One of the most important nuances training develops is the commitment to building self-efficacy, which typically comes from well-traversed challenges.

Similarly, you can train yourself to rely on and have access to your best even with you have very little around you. You can put everything you need in a tiny bag, a bag just big enough to get you out of trouble when you need to. Only the helpful and essential can go in it!

There is something intensely liberating about this, but it goes beyond the practical. In learning to be disciplined about what you carry with you, you also learn the discipline of knowing what to keep in your mind to carry you forward. Necessity helps you learn to strip down the white noise and the stuff that weighs you down.

Drop or shift

Drop

Imagine yourself standing around some of the big challenges and sources of depletion in your life – things you've labelled as boulders because you've allowed yourself to see them as things that block your way to thriving.

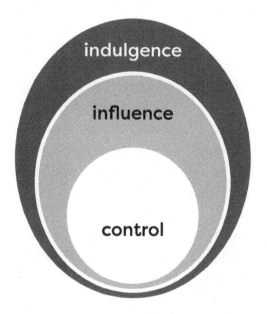

Accept that you have become exhausted running around the same exploratory loops, trying to change or understand things. Some of these challenges are there to be learned from, but it's time to put a stop to the unrelenting circumnavigation of the boulders you've grown attached to. It's time to drop these things. How do you drop them?

If this is something you can control or influence, what is stopping you from engaging in solving it?

The response to this question is usually related to time, energy or resources. If that is the case, you have two options:

1. Decide to reallocate resources and summon support so you can address this challenge and invest in creating a meaningful shift.
2. Ask yourself, 'Is this something that matters most? Is this something that matters now?' If this isn't something that matters now, choose to put it aside, knowing that if it continues to matter, it will stay with you and you will summon the resources to address it at a more appropriate time. If this is something that matters most, then revisit the ways in which you are approaching the challenge. Perhaps you need to replan your approach?

If the challenge is something that is outside of your control, accept that travelling around it on yet another exploratory loop is unlikely to be productive.

Without judgement, ask yourself, 'Why does this affect me so much, even though it is something I can do nothing about?' How can you better address the need that underpins your dedication to this challenge?

If you can't find a cause to engage with and address in order to minimise the demands of this challenge, allow yourself to put it to the side and focus on something you can control and influence. The likelihood is, if this uncontrollable challenge matters so much, it will remain available for you to engage with later. For now, the very best you can do is regain some confidence and energy from engaging with what you can influence and change.

Shift

If there are things you can't drop, try to shift the way you think about them. For me, this included things like:

- traffic on my commute
- endless piles of laundry
- the mess that just happens all by itself when you are raising a child
- the frustration I feel when my husband asks, 'What are we having for dinner?

The shift here came when I said to myself, 'Wow! You are one lucky little ninja!':

- Stuck in traffic? You have the freedom to move and the vehicle to move with on roads that can take you to your destination. Lucky!
- You can do your laundry? You are so lucky to live in a developed country, own a washing machine, have access to water and electricity – and you have items to put in the washing machine. Wait, you and your family have access to a change of clothes? So lucky!

- You have mess and a place to contain it in? That means you have a roof over your head and the confidence that that same roof will be there for you tomorrow. Your kid has clothes and toys? Blessed!
- You get to have a choice about what you can eat? You have readily available access to sustenance. So very lucky!

Easy right? And yet it takes daily practice.

Our brains are comforted by habits and norms, especially when we feel we fit within those norms.

When it comes to grit in your shoe and boulders in your mind, it takes deliberate action, awareness and persistence to disrupt the depleting normative expectations, to align and re-align our narrative and to broaden our scope to thrive.

It's essential that we learn to unlearn patterns of behaviour that we recognise as destructive or depleting. When you invest a little bit of curiosity into the process of changing your mind, the exercise becomes a little easier. More of your resilience remains available when you've unlearned those unhelpful patterns.

Tool: Connect 5

Let's practise how we adapt and evolve our approach to some of the triggers that deplete our resilience.

Think of one of your triggers or one of the things that depletes your resiliences. This might be an event, a recurrent thought, a set of specific circumstances you keep battling with, or even another person.

Using the examples below, complete the activity in the following sequence:

1. *Start by listing the trigger then walk yourself from 1 to 5 in a sequence down the dotted line.*

2. *Now consider the best case scenario – your ultimate, positive outcome. Here, jump up to the dashed line and start with the end (step 5) in mind. Describe that ultimate scenario.*

3. *Now go to step 1 on the dashed line. How could this same trigger be seen as a positive opportunity? Walk your way up the dashed line from 1 to 4.*

4. *If the dashed line is too much of a stretch for now, experiment with the bold line. What would it look like if you allowed yourself to observe this event or trigger with resilient neutrality? What would it look like if this trigger no longer affected you?*

5. *Start with the end in mind (step 5) by describing this outcome. Then walk your way from step 1 to 4 in a sequence.*

1 Interpretation (i.e. threat, opportunity or observation?)

2 Physiological impact: what does your body feel and where?

3 Response: how do you think/feel/act?

4 Outcome of response?

5 End result?

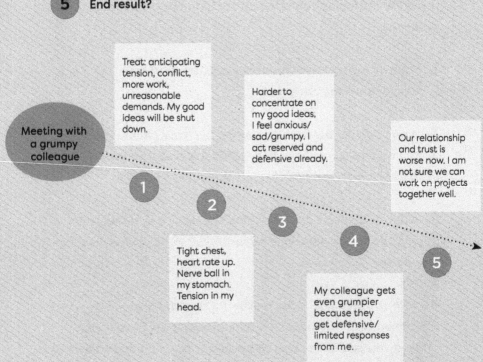

Meeting with a grumpy colleague

1 Treat: anticipating tension, conflict, more work, unreasonable demands. My good ideas will be shut down.

2 Tight chest, heart rate up. Nerve ball in my stomach. Tension in my head.

3 Harder to concentrate on my good ideas, I feel anxious/sad/grumpy. I act reserved and defensive already.

4 My colleague gets even grumpier because they get defensive/limited responses from me.

5 Our relationship and trust is worse now. I am not sure we can work on projects together well.

1 Interpretation (i.e. threat, opportunity or observation?)

2 Physiological impact: what does your body feel and where?

3 Response: how do you think/feel/act?

4 Outcome of response?

5 End result?

We stayed on track and did not escalate tension. Finally able to make traction and focus attention on the project issues we were there to address, rather than make it personal.

Calm. The situation has no impact on me. How others act is not in my control.

Meeting with a grumpy colleague

1   **2**   **3**   **4**   **5**

Observation: this is a situation I have encountered many times before. I don't have to be drawn in to the tension. My aim is to contribute in the best way I can and keep my own state of calm intact.

My thoughts are clear and I am focused on what I want to achieve. I act in a measured way but I am open to what we need to discuss today.

My demeanour made it clear that I was there to focus on the project. I communicated my ideas and made an impact on the project.

1 Interpretation (i.e. threat, opportunity or observation?)

2 Physiological impact: what does your body feel and where?

3 Response: how do you think/feel/act?

4 Outcome of response?

5 End result?

We have aligned each other's expectations and learned so much more about each other.

Excited! Energised. Curious.

5

4

3

2

1

Meeting with a grumpy colleague

Opportunity: this is a relationship I want to grow and strengthen. I will invest my curiosity today in finding how we can best align and support each other.

My mind is filled with great ideas on how we can move forward with the project. I feel strong and open. I act confidently and kindly. I am more patient. I feel empathetic. I know how committed they are! I am open to understand them better.

I have a thriving relationship with my colleague. I feel like a better human for having given them a chance to freely communicate their wants and needs without judgement. They are now my ally too and are supporting me. We have been able to have HUGE positive impact on projects together. This has made our whole team happier and increased trust and productivity across the board.

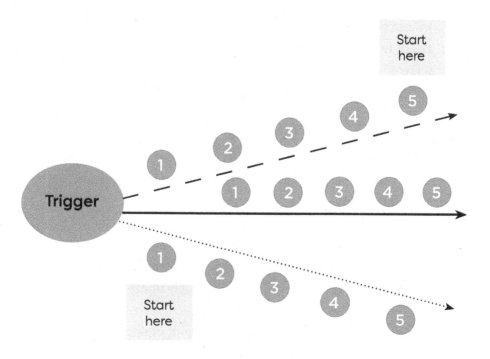

The angle to your pivot

Curiosity allows us to pivot to the positive. A lot of the time when we are dealing with stress, setbacks, trials or loss we find that our relationship with the pivot point or the event that causes us to pivot only changes in terms of time – the time that has passed or our physical distance from the memory.

Time passes but it only heals if we let it. No matter where we go, the memories and sense of self associated with the trigger stay with us. To be resilient, we have to travel lightly and pack the essentials that will enable us on the journey ahead. So that we can be resilient, we need to be mindful of the meaning we attach to our experiences and be deliberate about what we select to take along with us on our journey. It isn't always easy or simple, but it is essential.

Resilience, if we get it right, offers more than an effective response in the moment and healing after the event. It is not just there in relation to an event or a pivot point. Those are just reference points we describe our resilience by.

If we get it right, resilience is in in the gains we make from every encounter in our lives – in the cumulative gains from all exposures – whether they be good, bad, ugly or not-yet-labelled.

To pivot effectively we need to have a point of reference. A sniper will tell you, 'Where your eyes go, the rest of you follows.' We have to be clear on what we aim to and be ready to take the angle needed to hit that target. When we think about pivots, we think of them as drastic changes that move us in a completely different direction, but they are not that at all. Pivoting is merely moving from one thing to the next.

There is a vast difference between survival and resilience, and grit is only a component to resilience and one that can sometimes do more harm than good.

Making it to the other side of your predicament untacked can sometimes be the most resilient thing, but equally, it can be the least resilient.

PART 4
DRIVE

12. Purpose precedes drive

Awareness fuels resilience by allowing you to stand firm feet on the ground, eyes, mind and heart wide open; belonging grounds you; curiosity allows you to explore ways in which you might surmount obstacles. Drive is the final step in the resilience flow. It relies on you maintaining a healthy resilience baseline and allows you to sustain commitment to your goal.

Resilient people rely on drive to sustain their motivation and keep going day after day, trial after trial. When they fail or trip up, drive sees them bounce forward better than when their predicament found them. Drive is the reason why resilient people remain committed to being better always, whilst others make a habit out of giving up. Following loss, in the absence of drive some of us can let our joy and potential shrink to oblivion, withdrawing from the world. In contrast, resilient people grow greater compassion and generosity.

Is drive an innate characteristic that some of us have and others don't? If drive is developed, what sits behind it and how can we get more of it?

We all have access to the switch for drive at our disposal.

However, drive is not a switch you can just turn on. It is something that has to be worked on.

You need to be driven in order to persevere in the direction of healing, learning and thriving. There are two key reference points you need to know when it comes to drive:

1. Purpose precedes drive. You cannot expect to be driven if the goal ahead is not clear or captivating for you.
2. So that your drive sustains you and doesn't burn you out, you have to be unapologetic about maintaining your equilibrium.

Sacho

As a young boy growing up in Bulgaria, Sacho learned to view things from a different angle. His family had moved back to their village just outside of Sofia, where all five of them lived in a tiny room.

Sacho's childhood was full of adventure. He and his brother discovered a passion for science and physics because those were the only books in the village library that were free to borrow.

A mobile outdoor movie theatre would visit the village in the summer months. They would always show a few short science advancement films in between the propaganda infomercials. Sacho's family couldn't afford tickets to the movies, but that didn't deter him and his brother.

The screen was perched up in front of the school building, leaving space for paying viewers to sprawl across the yard. But right on top of the school roof there was a spot where Sacho and his brother could watch the movies for free. Their brains quickly became adapted to watching the screen in reverse. The risk of climbing up on top of the building made their minds that much more alert and ready to soak up the information shared in the films.

Sacho's love of science eventually led him to Star City in Moscow – the headquarters of the Russian space programme, where he trained to become an astronaut. His family profile didn't fit the Communist ideal, so Sacho didn't make the final cut. His passion for the skies remained undimmed so he returned to Bulgaria, where he served as a combat pilot for 20 years.

When he wasn't flying fighter jets, Sacho pursued his passion for hang-gliding. Realising the cost of importing hang-gliders made them unattainable to Bulgarians, he developed an affordable local brand instead, thereby creating many jobs and opening up the skies for more pilots to follow in his footsteps.

As a test pilot Sacho had more accidents then he could count. One of these accidents shattered his right arm. His doctors had advised him that he would never be able to enjoy his long standing passion for training in gymnastics again. Rather than sinking into despair, Sacho spent the next three months in his hospital bed gradually building his strength through mobility exercises. Eight months after the accident, Sacho walked into his doctors office on his hands. With a smile on his face, he said to his doctor, 'Never say never!'

Sacho had learned to defy the odds from an early age: the odds of a child from his background achieving academically and excelling professionally; the odds of him regaining his strength after body-shattering incidents; the odds of him returning to the skies after near-death test missions. But Sacho never worried about the odds. He was too busy chasing his dreams and his purpose.

Sacho had learned that humans are innately blind to the abundance of opportunities around them. He also knew that limitations were mere suggestions designed to give him a breather while he reconsidered and adjusted his approach towards his goals. This is why, when he was well into his forties, he didn't even consider the odds of succeeding when he decided to immigrate to New Zealand.

He had grown fed up with the corruption and political upheavals in Bulgaria, so he invested most of his family's savings into buying a plane ticket, not intending to use the return leg of the trip. He packed a hang-glider, an extra pair of jeans, a couple of tops and a tonne of curiosity. He'd decided he was going to attend a hang-gliding competition, then never leave. His purpose now was to secure a safe new home for his children in a place where they would be free to pursue their dreams.

The odds nearly got him this time. For months, Sacho applied for jobs with no success. His expertise, capabilities and potential were difficult to place. His enthusiasm never wavered, but he worried that he might never be accepted in this new country.

In the space he had to consider how to translate his thoughts in English, he would observe the micro expressions and tiny glitches that flashed involuntarily across the faces of his interviewers. He could see their brains scanning him.

His accent and underdeveloped language skills were causing them to strain their ears as they leaned forward to make sense of his words. But then he'd watch them lean back away from the intensity of his delivery.

Maybe they thought his message wasn't worth hearing because he didn't speak well. Maybe they confused Bulgaria with Bosnia, where a war was raging at that time, and thought he was somehow dangerous. Maybe they thought he was lying about some of the things he said he'd done as they seemed almost impossible.

The world where Sacho came from was rich with reasons for his defiance, for pushing right past what others thought was possible. But these reasons were far less visible in the world he so desperately wanted to be a part of now. In fact, he wasn't sure these same reasons existed here, at least not in a way he could easily recognise. The people around him now seemed genuinely nice.

'Nice' was uncommon in the world he'd left behind as it signalled weakness. There you had to watch your back. Here niceness was the norm.

People here seemed softer and moved more slowly. They would smile at strangers. If they'd experienced the brutalities Sacho had come to know throughout his life, then they were expertly hiding their scars.

Sacho understood that when people are exposed to something new or different they typically race back to what they already know, rather than pausing and discovering the new. This switch away from an opportunity to discover and towards confirming biases infuriated Sacho because he knew people were missing out on a chance to discover and learn from one another.

Sacho understood that unless people have had the chance to condition and practise curiosity, their minds were wired to race through the pages of existing references they had already collated. They would compute whether this new thing or person fitted in the familiar/safe/good or unfamiliar/dangerous/bad box. The haste of their days left no room for anything in-between.

Through all of his experiences, Sacho had learned that the most extraordinary opportunities for learning, connection, shifting and growing are typically hidden in plain sight. Just past the biases and preconceived notions rests the possibility to create the extraordinary. His entire life had been a manifestation of this.

In each of his unsuccessful job interviews, Sacho felt his presence invite the amygdalae of the gathered brains to do a quick dance with fear. They would scan him for potential threat before rating how worthwhile interaction with him might be. Then they would decide when to divert the conversation to 'Maybe next time' and 'Goodbye'.

Then one day, he didn't hear 'Maybe next time'. He got the job with only days to spare before his visa expired. The relief was overwhelming. Sacho had never felt this overwhelming mix of relief and gratitude before. Finally, he had secured a job in New Zealand – a job that would help him provide a safe future for his family and give his children much greater freedoms to pursue their dreams.

Sacho observed his emotions, trying to make sure they didn't take over his composure. He watched his body and mind, observing them fighting and sinking into waves of different emotions. He rode the waves, watching as they rose and dissipated. Relief.

He did not want the waves of relief to be seen by others. People who have not been privy to Sacho's journey to this moment would surely have seen his feelings as disproportionate. After all, this was just a job for which he was well overqualified.

He felt his muscles straining, trying to contain the mix of emotions. Suddenly, he heard the tones of his beloved acoustic guitar coming from deep within his memory bank. He could not help but smile as his internal soundtrack stole the focus from his new boss's instructions.

Pink Floyd's 'Fearless' quietly echoed through his mind, opening the walls around him, making his heart swell. 'How fitting,' Sacho thought, as he tried to make his grin fit with what was happening around him.

Anchor in your purpose

No matter the challenges he had confronted, Sacho's resilience could only be as strong as his purpose. He never ignored the magnitude of the challenge that stood in front of him. However tricky his predicament, he knew it was just a current state. This realisation alone gave him confidence. When things were tricky, 'as is' (the current state) was far less important than what was 'to be' (the desired state).

His resilience would always endure when Sacho was clear on his desired state. He always ensured that he had his sight set on his vision for the future; that this desired state, or 'to be', was meaningful, authentically aligned with him and captivating. It was in pursuit of purpose that he would sustain his drive to seek workarounds, explore alternatives, endure discomfort and sustain optimism, even when it felt like the gates to opportunity were shutting in front of him.

The realisation that purpose precedes drive and that drive is essential for resilience was shared amongst the special forces soldiers, top athletes, leaders, entrepreneurs and thrivers I encountered through my research.

When I started digging into the role of purpose in sustaining resilience in the SAS, for example, I kept coming across this response:

You have to ask yourself, how healthy is my forest of reasons?

Even if your purpose for persevering can be simmered down into one tidy statement, the extent to which it is aligned with your authentic self and how well you nurture your purpose will determine the strength of your resilience. In order for it to drive and sustain your resilience, your purpose has to hold deep, healthy roots within you.

To sustain your resilience, you have to know the reasons why the purpose you pursue is important to you. This is the 'forest of reasons'. For this forest of reasons to sustain you, you have to nurture it and keep it out of harm's way. This is done by making it less vulnerable to the inevitable drought of motivation, which occurs when you lose your energy to persevere, or are flooded by the conflicting priorities, doubts, demands and depletions we all experience as we traverse the unknown.

There is a simple starting point to this process, which challenges you to define your purpose; to make your purpose an audacious dream that captivates you, so that the sways and shifts of your present context – your 'as is' – is less likely to take away from it.

In defining your 'to be', or your audacious dream, you have to start with the end in mind. It has to be bigger than you. Make it big so that it grips you and makes you want to get out of bed in the morning. Then build the bridge back to your present moment, marking only the essential pivots that you will need to commit to, in order to pursue purpose.

Tool: My audacious dream

1. My distant dreams

2. What dreams need
to take shape mid-term
for my distant dreams
to materialise

3. What are the steps
I will take today,
this week, this month,
this year to step
into my dreams?

The three tests to purpose

So that your purpose sustains your drive and resilience, you need to take this idea of your audacious dream a little further. You need to know your 'why'. Resilience persists or broadens when you are clear and aligned with your 'why' or your purpose. Your purpose has to be beyond the mundane and the frivolous. There are three sub-themes to this. So that you stand a chance to ace your purpose, your purpose has to meet the ACE test:

- Authenticity – how aligned your purpose is with your personal values and beliefs.
- Clarity – how well you understand your purpose, and how well your purpose is integrated into your life.
- Elevation – how broad and enduring is your purpose?

Authenticity

Authenticity is measured by the extent to which what you commit or engage yourself with is meaningful and aligned with your personal values, motivations, vision for self and beliefs.

An authentic goal is one that is personally meaningful and well envisaged. It should also be able to be clearly articulated 'so that it holds through trials and setbacks'.

Make it personal. It has to be yours, so ground it in what matters to you. You cannot borrow someone else's purpose and expect it to sustain your resilience and drive in times of trial.

For example, your purpose might be to regain your health following a significant illness or loss of fitness because you've been neglecting your own needs. So that the purpose of regaining your health fuels your drive and sustains your resilience in the face of challenges, you need to make this purpose personal by including details.

As one of my interviewees shared, 'Your purpose will only go live if it is fuelled by your life.'

Make your purpose intrinsic to you, and make it positive and constructive. In this example, include the underpinning motivation for you to regain your health and fitness. This might be wanting to remain in the lives of your loved ones for longer or to inspire specific people in your life. Or it might hinge on your desire to do specific things that your health is preventing you from experiencing. Get specific on this. Give your purpose a wide net, woven with drivers that are unique to you.

Whatever your motivation might be, envisage the future states or experiences you are moving towards.

External drivers, such as wanting to look good for others, or fuelling the envy of an ex, are often fuelled by self-doubt, whereas internal ones are fuelled by self-belief and self-awareness. As one SAS member told me:

Impressing your critics or proving others
wrong may start you, but it will always eat
away at you, and you will fail yourself in the
end. If you try to tackle this type of challenge
from a negative starting point, you have
allowed the voices of your doubters, your
critics, to become your own.

Clarity

Make it specific. If you can't articulate your goals clearly or you
don't understand them, the gap between reality and your hopes
will make it impossible to persevere through the challenges you
face. It will also make it difficult for you to reframe those goals
should the need arise.

Taking on challenges with motivations that are not clearly
articulated or thought through is likely to result in loss of
commitment and motivation, leaving you hamstrung in
pursuing your goals. As one SAS member put it: 'Unless you
know and truly own the details of your "why", the challenges
out there will surpass your capabilities.'

Being really clear about your purpose will help serve your
resilience not only when you're responding to setbacks but also
when you're celebrating successes while working towards your
goals. It's much easier to maintain your commitment to a goal
if you're able to clearly understand it yourself.

When you encounter obstacles, clarity will help you to adapt and change as much as you need to in order to remain on your path to achieving your goals.

Elevation

Elevation is your ability to lift your purpose beyond the white noise of distractions in order to make it broad and enduring enough so that it is infallible. It's about lifting your 'why' so that it won't be taken away from you. As one interviewee put it: 'Unless your "why" is elevated, setbacks may take away your confidence, faith or ability to see yourself as capable of achieving your goal.'

Looking back on a deeply confronting personal experience that affected his family, one person I spoke to said: 'I had to quiet down my brain, consciously cut out the white noise from all the things that did not matter, or we could do nothing about. Our purpose needed to be beyond all that so we could persevere. It would have been easier to let go or let distractions distance us. But giving up in this way could have had devastating consequences. What helped us was focusing on our own big picture with clarity and creating different ways for that vision to come to life.'

Another person saw it like this: 'Life has a way to stir and question the vision you have created for yourself, the ideas you hold around who you are or what you want to be. You learn quickly; it is not the "what" that matters but the "why". There are many ways of making your "why" happen if you are clear on it and own it. If you want to do better for your community, you could do so by being a charity worker, a soldier, a nurse or simply a good neighbour. When you know your "why" you can change your vessel to get there without getting attached to that vessel. That is what resilience is all about.'

Be about it

Let's summarise this ACE approach to purpose. So that your purpose endures and sustains your resilience, you need to 'be about it, walk about it, talk about it'. This phrase was shared with me by one of the SAS operators I interviewed, but I kept discovering it as I observed how the most resilient among us designed and lived their purpose.

You need to be all about your purpose and your purpose needs to reflect all about you – your wisdoms gained, your unrestrained potential and your dreams. This means you need to be clear about the values and principles that guide you and these need to be in alignment with your thoughts, words and actions.

No matter the challenge, you ace your purpose when you believe it. This is because your purpose has become the thing you live and breathe. In the words of Anthony Hopkins:

Whatever you want to do, believe it, believe it, believe it. Even if you don't believe, play the game of belief, act as if you believe. That is power, that is sheer power.

As a result of obstacles you've encountered, you may have lost your belief that things can get better or that your purpose can become your lived reality. You *can* resurrect your purpose by giving it a deeper, clearer, higher meaning. The ACE approach, supported by mindfully selected habits, can shift you from hazy dreams, through clarity, to conviction. It can help you turn setbacks into lessons learned for greater resilience.

Tool: Be about it

Answer the following questions in sequence:

1. *What is my purpose?*
Review your responses to the 'My audacious dream' exercise on page 244.

2. *How does my purpose support and help me live my values?*
Review your responses to the 'Your values journey' exercise on page 148.

3. *How will my purpose change things for me, for others, for my environment?*

Now draw a picture or create a vision board that includes visual cues to your purpose. Get very clear with it. Using as much detail as you can, include images or symbols that captivate your intent.

- *What places does your vision involve?*
- *Where are you?*
- *What other people, stories, faces will this vision include?*
- *How do you stand in this vision?*
- *What is your body doing in it? Are you smiling? Pointing? Holding your arms victorious?*
- *Are you running or sitting on a beautiful beach?*

Make it as specific as you can. Revisit it as often as you need.

Once you know what your purpose is the process has begun, so it's time to get even more specific about your thoughts, feelings and actions.

Turn your purpose into a goal or goals. Now complete the G.R.O.O.W. questions below.

Goal:
List your goal(s).

Reality:
What is your current reality
in relation to your goal?

Obstacles:
What lies between where you
are and where you aim to be
in relation to your goal?

Options:
List alternatives and
strategies to help you
overcome your obstacles.

Ways forward:
Select the approach(es)/
options you will commit to
and any action within these.

What will I need to change for my purpose to come to life?

- Starting from today, create a timeline that includes objectives and milestones to be achieved weekly, monthly, yearly until you have reached your purpose or goals.

- Keep track of your progress. This means routines, behaviour changes and habits that move you in the right direction. Select the habits, routines and rituals that will serve you.

  Under pressure, you may default to negative habits that deplete your purpose and resilience. This process will help you to manifest your purpose and achieve the goals that underpin it.

- Watch your internal monologue. Suspend and disarm negative 'what if' questions, like 'What if I fail?' Instead, ask yourself positive 'what if' questions. For example, 'What if this is possible for me? What if this turns out right?'

Habits can be the engine for consistent growth or the rust that leads to degradation. You need to select, track, maintain and evolve the habits that will fuel and sustain your resilience for the journey ahead. Willpower is a limited resource and motivation may waver, so neither are particularly reliable. Meanwhile, recovery, capacity for thriving and, ultimately, resilience are not about willpower, but about habits.

Cue, routine, reward

Resilient people are driven by their purpose. They develop and integrate new habits that are congruent with their purpose. Your purpose will likely require you to form and integrate new habits into your life, too. While it can vary from person to person, on average it takes 66 days to turn a new habit into an automatic behaviour.

There are three parts to habit formation:

1. the cue
2. the routine
3. the reward.

Let's build on the earlier example of pursuing better health. One plan you might pursue to achieve this is going to the gym consistently.

Going to the gym is a decision we make – one that isn't as cued in us as our need to hydrate or eat to survive. As a decision, it has to compete with countless priorities in your day. As such, you are vulnerable because you have the capacity to rationalise why you shouldn't go. We are brilliant at talking ourselves out of doing difficult or new things. Remember, our brains love the familiar, even if it is not the optimal.

Cue

The cue is your prompt to activate a habit. They are reminders for your brain that ease you into a series of actions that then become your routine. For example, you may have a coffee machine at work. As you come in to the office in the morning, the smell of coffee might be your cue to grab a cup before you start work.

Cues tend to fit into the categories of location, time, other people, preceding actions and our emotional state. To help build the habit of going to the gym, set a sequence of times and days when you will commit to working out. Try to build a schedule that is reliable and predictable so your brain knows that, for example, 'on Mondays, Wednesdays and Fridays, I go to the gym at six o'clock.' The cue becomes the day and the time of day.

You can deepen your cues by using familiar music – your 'gym jams' – the route you take to the gym or a mantra to keep you going, such as 'I train my strength'.

Routine

You need to give yourself a nudge in the right direction. Don't leave your recovery or thriving to chance. That nudge might involve the routines that take the decision-making out of getting to the gym. Obstacles can be as benign as your alarm's snooze button, not knowing what to wear or not having an exercise regime.

- To build new habits you need to remove the obstacles.
- To avoid the snooze button, charge your phone away from your bed so you have to get up to turn your alarm off.
- If you find it hard to decide what to wear in the morning, set your gym gear out before you go to bed at night.
- If you don't have an exercise regime, talk to one of the trainers at your gym. They're usually happy to help write a programme for you.

Reward

When it comes to giving yourself a reward, if you love your morning coffee, save that for when you return from the gym.

Keep it simple

Tracking a lot of habits at one time can feel overwhelming, as we fall victim to decision fatigue, which then decreases our likelihood of success. There is a limit to how much we can store in our conscious minds or working memory at any time. As we work towards imbedding new habits and automating them, they are likely to demand more attention. Don't leave your purpose to chance. Simplify and ease your access to your goal by minimising the cognitive demand of your commitment to new habits. The best way to do this is to track no more than five habits each week.

13. Reduce the drag

Resilience lies in our ability to grow, evolve, learn and adapt following every exposure. Many of us have had experiences that demonstrate to us just how much resilience we can summon in a moment of need. To thrive, we need to demonstrate resilience not only in the way we engage with the challenges life throws at us, but the challenges we select for ourselves in the commitment to evolving our lives and potential.

Brian

Years into my resilience research, I met 'Brian', who would say, 'As far as resilience is concerned, there are two kinds of people – lifers and markers.'

Like me, he believed everyone could gain and sustain access to the extraordinary through resilience. However, Brian had observed that some people practise their resilience daily. These were the 'lifers'. Others, according to Brian, would put their lives on hold as a result of one remarkable event. He called this group 'markers'.

Though both groups had survived remarkable trials, lifers had gone on to evolve and seek new challenges, while markers continued to retell the story of their trial and survival, define themselves by their past and hold back on new challenges.

Brian would caution: 'Resilience has to be about more than a one-off story good enough to rehash at the local pub; the story that opens up with "Did you know that back in 1962, Johnny was …".'

These sorts of moments are significant but remain just markers; moments flagged in time. Unless they lead to some place greater, unless they are deliberately utilised to pivot and grow us through subsequent challenges, their colours will fade. Brian called these the 'has-been' resilience stories.

As a kid in New Zealand, Brian often spent his weekends with his grandparents. He looked forward to a weekend ritual with his grandad, a World War II veteran. Every Saturday, they would visit the local RSA and catch up with his grandad's mates from the war.

As a young boy, Brian cherished these visits. He felt he was in the company of superhumans. He had become part of this group of heroes who told remarkable stories of survival, bravery and camaraderie. Brian pretended he was there for a glass of lemonade and a few hot chips, but these were just his excuses for being at the table where his grandad and his veteran mates relished telling the same stories. After a while, Brian realised that the sequence of these stories was perfectly predictable. He found comfort in knowing what would happen next.

When one by one, the heroes he had grown with became the veterans who had passed, this sequence formed a painful realisation for Brian. As their individual stories were recounted at their funerals, Brian had a unique timeline in his mind in which he'd hear in his head the preceding and following stories he'd heard at the RSA.

When it became his grandad's time to pass, Brian was serving in the military. The pain of losing his granddad was piercing and intense. However, Brian felt an even greater pain than the loss of his grandad – the fear that, after the war, his grandad had never really lived.

At some point, Brian had developed the feeling that these extraordinary humans had, over time, become a one-hit wonder. It hit him that their lives, like their eulogies, had been written up a lifetime before their actual passing. Yes, most of the RSA group Brian knew had had long lives after the war. But, for the vast majority, life after the war was hidden in the trenches of the past. It was as if they had decided that there was only that much one could live through and survive in a lifetime; that the extraordinary had already happened and the rest of it was 'hide, wait and see until you die'.

They had forever remained those 20-something heroes of a war they didn't really understand. They ceased being active participants and influencers in their own lives and were, at best, passive observers and passengers en route to the inevitable end. Their stories had not evolved or been unpacked. It was agonising for Brian that, after the war, they were not heroes. They were simply men who had once done something heroic. But that, Brian knew, was just what human bodies and minds were designed to do in the extremes.

The men he had grown to love and admire were stunted by unresolved trauma. Reliving trauma without healing and resolving it stunts us. Reliving past failure or failing to commit to our vision because of setbacks does the same, stunting us in pain, fear, worry and rumination.

'There is always something,' Brian would say. It took me years to realise this was not a phrase to signal despair but instead hopefulness and opportunity. The realisation that as long as we live, there is a greater resilience opportunity ahead of us; something to be done, to learn, something new to pivot towards. That something may be as tiny as our own attitudes or perceptions. However, it is in those pivots where the greatest change exists.

This is why, in his later years, Brian remembered the RSA heroes with not only admiration but also sadness in that it appeared to him their lives, their capacity for exploring the extraordinary, had frozen in time. After years of service with the military, he decided to change careers and serve in a different way as a grief councillor. His motivation was fuelled by the realisation that so many of us appear to freeze our access to the extraordinary in time.

Resilience is not a one-off wonder. For us to sustain pressure, grow and evolve from it and thrive, we need to embrace resilience continuously.

Brian had many wonderful ways of inviting people to explore and grow from their past, especially the shreds of past some of us bury deep in the layers of our memory. Brian would say, 'When you try to shut out a chapter of your life without reading and processing it, you are committing to hearing about it from your mind, like an incessant rant for the rest of your life.'

The most depleting thing you can do is avoid the pain that comes from your experiences. In a space of resilience, avoiding pain also means rejecting the possibility of growth.

We have all heard about post-traumatic stress but many of us haven't had the opportunity to appreciate the power that sits inside post-traumatic growth. Post-traumatic growth occurs when you find a way to take new meaning from your experiences in order to live your life in a different and better way. The opportunities for growth are abundant in every challenge or trial we overcome or learn from.

Travel lightly

One of the models Brian used to help others process the challenges they were dealing with comes from the work of the Swiss-American psychiatrist, Elisabeth Kübler-Ross. A pioneer of studies into death and grief, Kübler-Ross developed the stages of grief model, which has since become widely used for helping individuals, teams and organisations in managing change. The model focuses on the stages of denial, anger, bargaining, depression and acceptance. Below is a more detailed version that reflects the wider responses we may have to significant change or challenges in our lives.

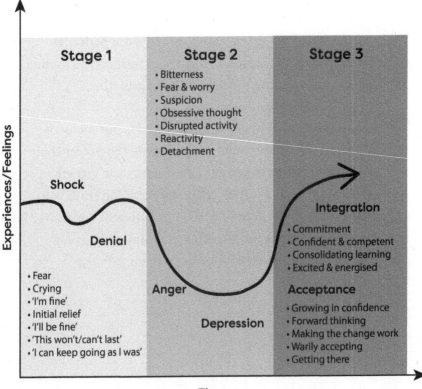

This model purports that, when confronted with significant change or challenge, most of us travel a line across these stages. There are two key takeaways from this model that apply to building resilience:

1. Don't avoid the feelings of the challenge or confronting experience. To heal from it, we have to feel it first. We all have unique challenges and resilience journeys, however, some of us try to swing to acceptance and integration, desperately hoping to avoid the weight of the negative emotions that come with processing our experience. We imagine that we don't have to traverse the pit, only to realise that the longer we leave it, the sharper the fall will be. Left unattended, these emotions find a way to remain in our lives, obstructing our way to the future.

2. Don't get stuck! Sometimes we may get stuck in the pits of anger and depression, which causes us to hesitate before climbing back out. Resilience lies in seeking to find the resources, support and energy you need to reach acceptance, integration and commitment to the new.

Brian also challenged the linear thinking of our western culture when it comes to overcoming challenges and setbacks. This thinking suggests that there is a line on which our journey from challenge to growth sits.

Past ⟶ Present ⟶ Future

The assumption sometimes is that once we get to that better state, the future will always hold us strong. The hope is that we will move from one struggle to infinite thriving, but that is seldom the case. Life is there to challenge us, continuously. The good news is that if we accept the challenge of life, we will gain learning and grow in ways that may never be afforded if we avoid challenges.

The creation story

The Māori creation story is the oldest philosophy of Aotearoa New Zealand. It is powerful in explaining the journey to healing, growth and learning, and bringing about transformation. I learned of this story from one of my SAS mentors, who was guiding me in my practice of building resilience in our troops.

The journey begins with Te Kore – the great nothingness, the empty void. In Te Kore, there is nothing above and nothing below. In the context of resilience, this translates to the experience of shock and the numbness you may experience when you confront an abrupt or unexpected change, loss or challenge that overwhelms you.

Time is suspended in darkness as if to illustrate a state of unrealised potential. However, Te Kore is also the realm of energy and pure potential. It fuels and creates the conditions for change. The space of Te Kore offers a challenge and an opportunity. No matter how confronting it may seem to achieve this amid Te Kore, your role is to carefully choose and commit to your intention. This is so you can galvanise the emerging potential towards the positive – acceptance, recovery, learning and thriving – rather than the negative.

Te Pō is the next phase. From the empty void of shock or impact emerges the realm of perpetual night. Te Pō is flooded in darkness. Fear, doubt, sadness and regret may live here, but so may hope. Movement and awareness of being emerge, as do the beginnings of change towards the realm of becoming and the possibilities of learning, growing and transforming. The pathway through the darkness symbolises the varying stages of transformation where new narratives, ideas or opportunities are identified.

Finally comes Te Ao Mārama, the world of light, coming into being, flourishing. It is our place of thriving, where learning is integrated into supporting an even more resilient version of ourselves. This place of light is impermanent in life. New challenges will face us, and from them will emerge greater opportunities.

How can these stages of creation guide you on your resilience journey?

- Each of these phases are a passing moment in time. Each of these experiences – the challenge, the exploration and the light and thriving – have a great deal to offer for resilience.
- If you avoid the discomfort and pain as well as the learning and growth following challenges, you commit to circumnavigating the same space, failing to see all that may lie ahead or outside of it.

- Load, strain, challenge – this is the language of our cells. We are wired for them, but many of us avoid them. Instead, we should sit with them, learn from them, grow through them – this is the resilient pathway.
- Learn to sit in discomfort as that's where growth happens.

To be resilient, you must accept that the journey may be arduous at times. Every new exposure offers learnings and opportunities.

The aim is not to avoid challenges, but to instead use what you have learned so that you don't go deep into despair after you've confronted the unforeseen. If we gain the learnings offered by challenges, then the dip may be normal but less deep.

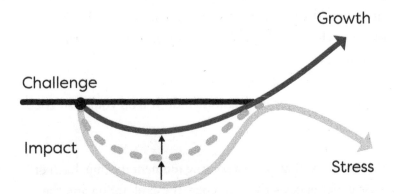

Acceptance and readiness

In the words of one SAS member: 'So that you can recover and grow, you first have to have the capacity to accept and understand your points of failure, the source of your predicament; to accept what has taken place.'

Resilience happens when you can turn this acceptance into your vehicle for growth. Resilience means moving forward better prepared than when your setback found you. Acceptance is the key to growth and movement in the direction of resilience, and it ultimately underpins your broader readiness for taking on the journey ahead.

The capacity to evolve, learn and be prepared continuously is key to resilience. According to one of the SAS soldiers I interviewed: 'The approach that serves you well today may be your undoing tomorrow unless you pay attention and keep a hungry mind.'

If you do your utmost in everything you engage with, whether you succeed or fail becomes less relevant, as you will grow from it.

One SAS member explained how what he was exposed to through his work supported his resilience by broadening his capacity for acceptance and readiness: 'You begin to see the habit of staying too long with the feelings of loss, pain or failure as indulgent. You move from a mindset fixed on fear, and you learn instead to look up, around and within so that you make new ways for the outcomes you aim for. And then you go forward with an open heart and in the fullness of your mind.'

Focus on acceptance is critical in supporting your confidence in tackling complex demands as it enables you to broaden and sustain your resilience in times of trial. One interviewee commented: 'To be resilient and capable in dealing with the big challenges, you have to come prepared with all the basics and to feel prepared to the best of your abilities.'

This happens by accepting, learning and growing through every experience – the good, the bad and the ugly.

Perseverance

Perseverance is a practised attitude to be developed rather than an innate trait.

Resilience is a quality to be continuously nurtured and conditioned. It starts with perseverance in the willingness to step forward into new challenges. In the words of one interviewee: 'Even in the darkest of moments, there is always something more to be done or, at least, something new to be learned. No matter your predicament, this mindset triggers you to ask, "What if?" once more. Your win could be in that extra second; in that extra step you take.'

One person I spoke to commented: 'At first, building the appetite to push past setbacks or pain can feel like practising going through a concrete wall – it sucks. You want to pause, to stop completely. But when you make learning and improvement your aim, you understand that most obstacles are self-imposed, at least in the attitude you take. You choose to persevere.'

Another explained: 'When you condition perseverance, curiosity and the pursuit of your best replace fear.'

Resilience is underpinned by the desire to pursue challenges rather than avoid them; to learn from and lean into the new rather than stick with the familiar; to improve self always, rather than prove yourself right; to imagine better always, rather than ruminate on the bad. In all these areas, resilience demands perseverance. The measuring unit for perseverance is consistency.

14. Guard your equilibrium jealously

Viktor Frankl, the holocaust survivor and world-renowned psychotherapist sought to help his patients find ways to better answer their most important existential questions. His mission was to help his patients change their relationship with suffering and increase their capacity for a life of meaning. I mentioned Frankl's impact on my own work on page 5, but reiterate here the idea of the space between stimulus and response, and the power within that space to act resiliently.

If we pay attention, we get to encounter the space Frankl speaks about. Some of us may hold memories of times when we have seized the opportunity in that space between stimulus and response. Rather than reacting sub-optimally or habitually, we have made a deliberate choice to respond and engage with our challenge deliberately and to influence the outcome for the better.

Many of us have experienced crucible moments and, within them, witnessed what we are capable of. However, one defining moment, one choice or even a few pivot points are seldom enough for building an enduring resilience. Resilience demands that we locate this space, the opportunity for us to meet the challenge and broaden our strengths, daily.

This can be seen in the lives of the people who choose to challenge themselves mindfully in every moment.

Resilience and the brain

The more you practise something, the more your brain changes. Every single neuron in the brain makes 10,000 connections with other nerves and those links change based on the things that we do most.

When someone learns something new, a pathway is temporarily forged by a chemical surrounding the neuron. If they then practise that same thing day in, day out, those chemical changes become structural. Over time, the neurons will actually change shape and shift their position. As the pathways become more fixed, connections between different brain regions strengthen.

By practising the things we want to get better at, we improve at them and we lay down the neural frameworks to be able to continue improving.

A memory is two neurons having a familiar conversation. Repeated, that conversation becomes a pattern we can follow without thought – like tying our shoelaces or riding a bike.

Memories tend to stick around when there are strong emotions attached to them. This is because emotions and the nervous system go hand-in-hand. The nervous system is in charge not only of processing our emotions but of deciding how we react to them. Sometimes our emotions can be so strong that they can overload our systems.

Sudden danger, crisis, fear and how your brain interprets them can quickly become the greatest threat. Your response can take total control of your mind and body. As a result, we can end up completely paralysed by our own emotions. When the amygdala is in charge, logic and reason shut down. No signals can reach what runs totally on instinct and emotion.

Aristotle once said we are what we repeatedly do. In that case, excellence can become a habit. The same applies to resilience. It, too, can become a habit. To build it, we must stay calm in the moment.

Fear is a very powerful protective mechanism for us. It is an enormously powerful adaptation that helps us internalise information and then allows us to respond to it quickly before the threat catches up with us. The trouble is we can form a habit out of fear, worry and anxiety, allowing them to spin us off balance and erode the benefits on offer for our resilience. If we don't find a way to maintain a sense of calm, we create a constant state of churn and angst, even in the absence of reason.

Calm inside the seconds

My father would say: 'The magic of resilience is the chain of events you form by the accumulation of seconds in which you choose to stay calm and act in full confidence that you can turn your faith around over and over again until you overcome.'

The more you train that calm inside the second, the greater your resilience baseline. It is clear to see why the power of the 'calm inside the second' was so engrained in my father's life. As a test pilot, he would have been conditioned to anticipate the opportunities that sat inside those decisive microseconds. His greatest moments and most significant achievements could easily be traced back to being calm inside the second.

The magic in my father is that he was able to translate these learnings to his life on the ground. It was as if every one of his moments in training as a test pilot had, incrementally, led to conscious, sensed, felt appreciation for the importance of paying close attention to his interactions with people, his environment and himself. I have observed that same characteristic in some of the most remarkable people I have met since.

This resilience habit does not prevent us from experiencing strain, but it ensures that when we feel the challenge of the moment, we experience it with less severity. It ensures that we are not blinded in the moment to the detriment of our goal or frozen in time to the detriment of our growth.

Just like Special Forces soldiers, my father relied on drills and instincts formed by repetition to the point where the best decisions were imprinted in a sequence stored in the muscle memory of every fibre of his body. For people who deliberately train for resilience in the specific context of their craft, these become trained reactions that carry them to optimal outcomes. For the vast majority of us, however, our reactions are not always optimal.

There are many meaningful and pivotal moments where our instinctual reactions are helpful and there are times when they are not enough or are even detrimental. Those are the moments that demand the mindful, deliberate pause Frankl spoke about. In these moments, we need to be able to rely on insight that can only be gained by being fully present, committed and engaged with the here and now.

Occasionally, the seconds between event and reaction feel borrowed. In these cases, you have to slice the second to make the microseconds your counting measure. Your body language, posture, glance, stance, breathing and how you orient towards these microseconds with every part of you will count towards the outcome of the encounter.

What goes on in these microseconds? Choicefulness – the decision to sustain commitment to your goal or vision in spite of feedback that might derail you like being overwhelmed, exhausted, fearful or the interference of negative emotions, habits or opinions.

Tool: Practise calm inside the seconds

When you are experiencing or preparing to confront a challenge, it is important to focus on first 'being' rather than 'doing'. This demands you find ways to be thoughtfully contemplative rather than emotionally reactive. Getting control of your thoughts and emotions can have a direct impact on your quality of life. It can change the way you interact with the world around you. The easiest and most effective way to regain calm is through your breath. Here's a simple exercise that you can do every day.

1. *Select or create a calm environment.*

2. *In this environment, take a deep breath into your stomach. Breathe out. Repeat this 10 times.*

3. *Take note whether there is any difference in your state after taking these breaths.*

4. *Repeat this exercise when your stress level is slightly elevated. To do this, try raising you pulse rate by running up some stairs or jogging on the spot for a few minutes. Again, note any changes to your state before and after taking the breaths.*

5. *Repeat the exercise when you are in a more emotionally uncomfortable situation. Be vulnerable. Speak from the heart. Be truthful. Say the things that are real for you. When you do this, notice your state. Pause, then take 10 breaths. Notice what happens to your state. Practise getting your breathing right when both physical and emotional consequences are on the line.*

Taking control of your physical and emotional state through something as simple as your breath helps you learn how your mind and body work. The things that challenge your resilience are seldom something you can plan for. While you cannot control everything that happens in your life, you can influence your experience of it and how you engage with it. Breathing is the easiest, most essential and impactful way to gain calm in the seconds. Conditioning this awareness allows you to condition access to your resilience.

Jonathan

One of the most remarkable entrepreneurs I have worked with, Jonathan impressed in countless ways. By the age of 30, he had established an empire that stirred up one of the most competitive and rigidly framed industries on the market. He had achieved that through sheer determination, inquisitiveness and, most of all, his remarkable ability to genuinely connect and care for people. That genuine connection and caring was particularly uncommon in the cut-throat, sales-based industry he worked in. In that world, the only measure of success was how quickly you could push your competitor (aka your colleague) off their perch as top salesperson.

Jonathan had done just that, but as he was busy replaying the same recipe for success that had got him to becoming Jonathan version 1, all the while he was also trying to escalate to Jonathan versions 2 and 3.

He had no formal tertiary education, but he took pride in proving that it was possible to become an astonishing success by standing against the status quo. While he had felt largely neglected growing up, he had surpassed many others who'd had access to education in private schools and universities. Now, though, he wanted to pave the way so that anyone could pursue whatever they wished, unobstructed by whatever society prescribed as the way to success.

When he was in his late thirties, Jonathan's success had begun to intimidate him. He had gone on, trying to be everything to everyone, not realising that his scope for life was changing. He wondered whether all he had done had been just so he could make a point; whether he'd invested all of himself into simply proving that it was possible to turn failure into success, neglect into worthiness, poverty into wealth, restlessness into entrepreneurship. The only way he knew to be worthy was to slog, but he also knew he could no longer live this way.

He couldn't even locate his purpose, let alone thrive towards the next iteration of himself because he didn't have time to reflect. The family he had been blessed with saw him as a lovable stranger. He had provided for them and he had proven himself, but now he was repeating the only way he knew to feel worthy – grind, slog, rinse and repeat.

His motivation was disappearing. He knew he should feel love and excitement for all that he had built, but instead he felt nothing but the weight that came with getting there. He was beginning to experience detachment, anxiety and 'a sense of otherness'.

Jonathan was experiencing the effects of burnout. He had pushed himself way past any sustainable threshold and allowed himself to carry unbearable loads for too long. The habit of being 'stressed to the max' had defined his life as an adult and he knew he carried it as a badge of honour. There were no moments for recovery or respite in his calendar. By the time he realised that he was completely depleted, he couldn't even remember what fuelled him.

Equilibrium and oscillation

Stress, change and ambiguity take us as they find us. When we are depleted to our limits, something as subtle as a change of wind could trigger our undoing. Hence, the phrase 'the straw that broke the camel's back' is one many of us can relate to as, at some stage, we have continued to push forward on an empty tank.

The experience of depletion or burnout is less about the load we have carried and more about the opportunities to recover and refuel that we have failed to secure for ourselves.

The resilience heroes I have worked with would argue that in order to sustain your drive, you have to be unapologetic about maintaining your equilibrium. The specifics of what fuels and sustains each of us may vary. However, the overarching principles to adhere to are much the same.

The resilience heroes I have learned from are all capable
of maintaining significant loads and tackling enormous
challenges for prolonged periods of time. In order to do so,
they are also committed to knowing when to be what; when to
fight and when to rest; when to strive and when to reflect; when
to pursue restlessly, fully absorbed in their mission and when
to connect and ground with their surroundings. It is a balance
that they guard jealously. They maintain peak performance
through carefully nurtured access to their resilience.

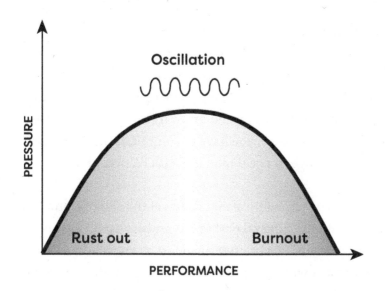

Oscillation is the careful and deliberate balance between pressure
and performance. The principle stipulates that if you don't have
enough pressure, your performance will lapse. You are likely to
experience rust out, typically accompanied by low motivation.

Rust out is a label used to describe our state when we feel unstimulated or unchallenged by the thing we are doing. When we are not captured by what we are doing, when it doesn't stimulate us, we typically become detached from it and unmotivated to continue on with it.

As Jonathan found out, your performance will also suffer if you have experienced significant pressure without respite. This leads to a different label, one commonly used to describe a mismatch between stress and performance – burnout. It leads to much the same results as rust out – loss of motivation because we have depleted our resources.

A good example of oscillation is a multisport event, such as the Coast to Coast. Imagine it being made up of sprints and restful recovery, spikes in activity and carefully orchestrated respite. To maintain resilience, you have to commit to the resistance and the challenge in equal measure with recovery.

Recovery is not something that comes at the end of a process, but rather it is an integral part of the process itself. The only way to evolve and maintain resilience is to know how to refuel and with what when the pressure is off. In periods of prolonged demand, this may require micro moments of the right fuel at the right time.

To know how to do this, first you have to know what fuels and sustains you.

Recover and refuel

There are countless models and approaches available to guide you towards maintaining your equilibrium. One of the most useful references I have come across is Te Whare Tapa Whā. The reference was developed by the Māori health advocate Sir Mason Durie in 1984 and describes health and wellbeing as a wharenui or meeting house with four walls. This Māori model suggests that to have strong and enduring resilience, the foundation and pillars that hold it together are all equally important. You must attend to them all.

The foundation is whenua – the land or your roots. This is where knowing the sources and fuel for your belonging come forth. The walls building your life on your foundation of belonging are tinana, your physical health, and whānau, the health of your family or social connections. The roof is made up of te taha wairua – spiritual well-being – and te taha hinengaro, your mental and emotional well-being.

Whether you consider yourself religious or not, spiritual well-being is essential. If you are religious, this may mean ensuring you make the time for your religious faith and community in your place of prayer. If you are not religious, this may mean consistent access to the things that bring you joy, fuel you and give you a sense of hope. For some, this may be as simple as time in the outdoors and in nature. What matters is that you have consistent access to whatever it is that fuels you and re-energises you.

Tool: Your current resilience baseline

Te Whare Tapa Whā

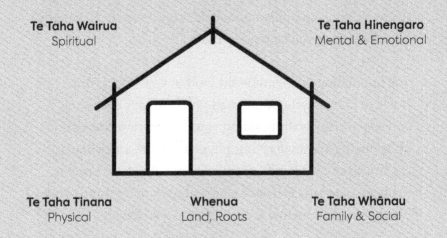

Te Taha Wairua
Spiritual

Te Taha Hinengaro
Mental & Emotional

Te Taha Tinana
Physical

Whenua
Land, Roots

Te Taha Whānau
Family & Social

Let's start with an honest self-assessment. This is entirely subjective, as what fuels and sustains you is all about the unique, irreplicable you! Importantly, it is not about an ideal you, but you as you are right now at this point in your journey to become a resilience hero.

To build up your baseline, you need to know your starting point. On a scale of zero to 10, where 0 is 'poor, low or depleted in this area' and 10 is 'being at my best', evaluate your current resilience levels in each of the five areas of Te Whare Tapa Whā.

Where you scored yourself less than 10, ask yourself the following questions:

1. *What is keeping you from this element being at its full strength?*

2. *How might you get greater access to this source for your resilience?*

3. *If your usual or preferred way is difficult for you to access, what alternative ways might you have to meet those needs?*

Prioritising sleep hygiene

When it comes to managing our health, many of us neglect the very basics. However different we may be in the ways we fuel our resilience bucket, there is one essential factor that applies to us all – the quality of our sleep can determine whether our resilience baseline is robust or on the verge of collapsing.

Improving the quantity and quality of your sleep could be a game changer for your energy, vitality, health and resilience. The simple rule is you cannot be driven if you are depleted. Sleep gives you the biggest opportunity for better recovery. Sleep is essential for cognitive processing, reaction time and emotional regulation. Sleep deprivation can result in lapses of attention and judgement, as well as degraded decision-making with widespread consequences for longer term health and wellbeing.

Getting good sleep starts with setting the right conditions. Here are the essential basics to help improve your sleep.

Sunlight

The first part of building good sleep patterns involves getting sunlight. The sun is essential for stimulating the parts of the brain that help line up our circadian rhythms. The circadian rhythm regulates the sleep–wake cycle our bodies need to adhere to in order to remain healthy.

Exercise

Any form of movement is essential for your circadian rhythms. It also gets your body to appreciate that rest is needed to switch on and to be effective.

Cut back on sugary and processed foods

Many of us reach for sugary and processed foods when we are depleted. This is the exact time when our bodies require pure nutrients the most. After eating sugary or processed foods, you get a dump of insulin and then a sugar high, which isn't conducive to helping you sleep.

Proper hydration

At the cellular level, it's important to get hydration right, but as it relates to sleep, you need to hydrate throughout the day then limit your intake of water in the evening and don't drink anything with caffeine in it after 2 pm so having to get up to go to the toilet doesn't disrupt your sleep. The rule is you should drink around 35 millilitres of water per kilogram of your body weight. Try consuming this amount, gradually before 4 pm.

Mimic sundown

Over thousands of years, our brains have become attuned to sundown meaning it's nearly time to go to sleep, so give your ancient brain a little bit of help. Our televisions, tablets and phones emit a tonne of blue light, which deceives our brains into thinking that the day goes on and on. Neurochemically, the moment you have blue light on board, you're sending signals to your brain to stay up. This prevents your body from producing a neurochemical for sleepiness called melatonin. Get the TV out of your bedroom. If you can't do that, at least get the tablets and the phones out of your bed. If possible, charge your phone in another room and use an old-school alarm instead. Looking at your phone, which is a culprit for blue light for many of us, is a stimulant.

Create a cave-like environment

When you switch off the lights, make sure your room is as dark as it can be. If need be, invest in blackout blinds or curtains. If you have air-conditioning, set the thermostat to 20°C. Make your room as quiet as possible.

Have a pen and paper ready by your bed

Do you sometimes wake up in the middle of the night with thoughts racing through your head as if your mind is a motorway? If you are unable to shut these thoughts down and quieten your mind in that moment, scribble down your thoughts. Getting them out of your mind and onto the page leaves one less thing for your brain to try to retain.

Pair your pillow with deep sleep

Your bed is not for watching television or using your computer. Train your brain to know that when you're in bed, it's time for sleep.

Building your awareness of your sleep patterns and needs is the first step to tracking your recovery.

Unable to sleep?

If you can't fall asleep or you wake and are unable to go back to sleep, get out of bed. There is no point lying there while your mind is spinning. Instead, you need to get back to that process where you're beginning to shut down. Allow your brain the chance to realise your body needs some rest.

- Take note of anything that may be on your mind. Don't try solving it now, just park it on a note, so that it isn't on your mind.
- Pick up a book – preferably an easy read; something light.
- Remember, blue light is the enemy of sleep, so keep away from your phone, TV or any electronic devices that omit light.
- Focus on your breathing. Do 10 or more deep belly breathing cycles (see page 139).
- Commit to a quick progressive muscle relaxation (PMR) session (see following page).

Tool: Progressive muscle relaxation

1. *Sit in a comfortable position or, better yet, lie down.*

2. *Curl both your fists and tighten your biceps and forearms.*

3. *Gently and slowly roll your head around in a clockwise direction then roll it anticlockwise. Repeat several times.*

4. *Activate the muscles on your face by wrinkling your forehead, squinting your eyes and opening your mouth wide. Hunch your shoulders up towards your ears. Release the tension by lowering your shoulders and relaxing your face. Repeat several times.*

5. *Pull your shoulders back as you take a long, deep breath into your chest. Hold for a few seconds then release the breath and relax your shoulders. Repeat several times.*

6. *Straighten your legs then point your toes towards you. Tighten your shins. Hold. Relax. Straighten your legs then curl your toes, while tightening your calves, thighs and buttocks. Hold. Relax.*

Conclusion

Every one of us is meant to be the hero of our own journey through life. This journey we are on demands resilience, as it is the essential ingredient for our survival and our capacity to overcome and thrive in our lives. Resilience is something we all have access to in abundance. However, sometimes we go about getting to it in all the wrong ways.

Resilience is not necessarily about happiness or measures of success. Sometimes, resilience lies in deciding what we will let fail. It is not always about bouncing back or forward. Sometimes, resilience demands stillness; the ability to absorb rather than deflect the impact of what has taken place; the strength to face, process and accept it. But we must not get stuck.

To heal and thrive, we must face the challenges presented by life with eyes, minds and hearts wide open. We need to ground ourselves in the reality of our present moment, with our gaze fixed on hope, possibilities and the vision we have created for ourselves.

Life does not occur in the absence of change, but resilience is what allows us to turn change into an opportunity.

Our opportunity is to be better, always, not despite but because of what we have lived through.

The power of resilience – the stuff that makes it essential for us all – lies in its ability to make us better, stronger, more aware and more capable than we were when our predicament first found us. Life is designed to accommodate and absorb challenges, setbacks and even pain. The resilience opportunity that every exposure holds for us is in growing through our experiences.

Resilience is in the capacity to pivot to the positive, to better. In any situation, no matter how challenging, there can be learning and growth. There is always scope for healing and hope, no matter how confronting or depleting our trials.

In some cases, the test for resilience may be met by the realisation that we *can* make it to the next moment in our life. Sometimes, waiting for that heavy, all-engulfing moment of challenge to pass can demand superhuman capabilities. But we all have those.

Stress, change and ambiguity take us as they find us. When we are depleted what may have felt manageable can suddenly seem insurmountable. We may come to a place where we feel we don't have the energy to get the energy we need to fuel back any remnants of hope. When we feel overwhelmed, we need to remember that this moment will pass.

There is no hiding from the trials of life, but there is an immense opportunity in surmounting them in a way that sees us learn and grow. It is in making it through those moments that we get to discover just how much better we could be.

Resilience is not about grit or handling stuff way past our perceived point of tolerance. Resilience is in adapting – be that our capabilities or narratives for lives. Every new moment and experience holds possibilities. The possibility may lie in developing a deeper appreciation for life – compassion for others who travel on their own hero's journey, understanding of ourselves or potential to enrich the lives of others with our own learnings.

So that we can overcome and grow, we need to jealously guard our resilience resources. If we pay attention, sometimes what depletes our resilience is not the evidence of what has happened, but the interpretation we attribute to it and our prediction of how this may shape our journey ahead.

We may not always be able to avoid or remove all that depletes us. That's not how life is designed. If we haven't set the challenge for ourselves, life will do so for us. However, we can select what we engage with and how we do it, and, most importantly, what experiences and learnings we choose to pack with us for our journey ahead.

Every experience remains a part of our fabric for life. To move resiliently ahead, we need to mind the narrative we craft for our life. It is all in our hands, including evolving our perspectives or attitudes, and selecting and shaping our moods. We have the freedom to select how we engage even when we feel forced, constrained, depleted or stretched.

Resilience is fuelled or depleted by the choices we make in how we engage with our experiences – be they in the moments of trial or in the ways in which we choose to integrate them as we reflect.

Resilience for recovery, growth and thriving follows a cadence, a sequence, a rhythm – awareness, belonging, curiosity and drive. The ABCD resilience sequence is not a linear process but an evolving sequence of reference points that helps sustain and fuel our capacity for better. Resilience is in developing clearer awareness, deeper belonging, broader curiosity and stronger drive. Every one of these reference points is essential for resilience.

Resilience demands that we maintain awareness of ourselves and our context, not as we wish it to be or assume it is, but as it is – warts and all. This also means we are willing to recognise responses that may be inbuilt or habitual but destructive, and orient instead towards more adaptive, optimal responses.

Resilience demands we maintain or create access to enabling belonging – a reference we hold within ourselves that sees us worthy of taking on the challenge. A sense of belonging to our strengths, our potential for good, our worth – this is vital for resilience because belonging shapes the power and direction of our engagement with our predicament.

Curiosity can transform a sense of doom and woe into wonder, fear into focus on possibilities, rumination into anticipation. It allows us to seek rather than avoid challenges, and to transform the unsettling into the exciting.

To be resilient, we need to be driven. So that our drive sustains our resilience, it needs to be authentically aligned with the purpose only we can conjure for ourselves. When driven, a setback becomes an opportunity to pause and reflect; the seemingly impossible becomes plausible because we can build better.

This cadence to resilience – ABCD – applies to us all. However, we are all unique. To make it through challenges and ultimately thrive in a way that matters to us, we need to understand and create the precise conditions for our own resilience. The conditions we need to nurture our strengths and potential as we navigate trials vary in detail from person to person. But they may also change for each of us, as our lives change and evolve. We need to pay close attention, seek to understand, explore and reach out for what fuels us uniquely. We need to know the conditions that sustain our resilience. If we cannot find them, we can create them.

Our freedom to choose and build for better is entirely in our hands. Resilience gives us the power to reach out and claim that freedom. Doubt and fear only live in our minds, and they stay only if we let them.

In every change, crisis and experience, there are junctions. Every junction holds a proposition; an invitation to notice, select and commit to better, always. Resilience is in the cumulative growth and learnings we gain when we chose to commit to pursuing better.

Acknowledgements

We walk by and live amongst extraordinary stories of resilience daily. We sit, unknowingly, with a wealth of wisdom that can heal and evolve us. I believe that wealth's only worth is when it is shared for good. Many of us also sit in the crippling hold of fears, indecision, worry and rumination.

I wrote this book so that the moments and wisdoms I have witnessed and learned from can heal and bring more of us closer to thriving.

To Professor Kathryn Pavlovich, who has taught me how to contribute from a place of faith, strength and curiosity, thank you for sponsoring the most cathartic epiphany of my life thus far. Thank you for shining a light on curiosity, for the power of your grace, for your astonishing wisdom and the gift of your warmth.

To Dr Erica Seville who introduced me to the word 'serendipity' and continues to inspire me with what it means to be a conduit to knowledge, hope, connection and exploration.

To every entrepreneur, soldier, leader, survivor and thriver who has inspired this book, thank you for showing us the pursuit of something better and for demonstrating how to take a leap of faith and sit with both equanimity and restlessness in traversing this mighty journey of life. You are the extraordinary yet common resilience heroes who 'take the Golden Road to Samarkand' each day. There could be no better subjects, mentors, teachers or guides than those who have mastered the most important journey to resilience – the journey that unfolds within!

All journeys of importance start with wonder. Wonder allows us to accept that the pursuit of purpose must become the unescapable logic for the narratives of our lives. For this realisation alone, I am beyond blessed!

My father, Alexander Bojilov, a tireless explorer, a pure wonder himself, the truest nurturer of wonders for others, has shared with me the gift of wonder in every step I have witnessed of his life. Watching my father encourage wonder has blessed me with the agency, freedom and conviction to do good, to gift, to construct possibilities, even when none can be seen.

To the greatest wonder and gift of my life – my brilliant son. I admire and love you so deeply. The power of your joy for life, your strength of character, your unbridled curiosity and wisdom in knowing how to be you unapologetically is the superpower that drives me. You inspire all with your masterful, daily teachings on curiosity and resilience.

At crucial junctions, wonder needs grounding so that we, the wonderers, can navigate and weather the storms. We need True North, solid ground and the equipment to see us through.

I dedicate this work to my husband, who grounds me and offers me an unfiltered vision for better, always. As the quintessential minder of wonderers, my husband upholds the tenets to resilience in all aspects of life, delivers the sense of realism required for me to hold onto all that it takes to continue ahead. He knows 'what goes where in the order of life'.

Any journey worth pursuing is marked by crucible moments. The final such moment is defined by the experiences we get to have with those who choose to share our steps. To the remarkable Holly Hunter, Nic McCloy and the HarperCollins team – thank you from the bottom of my heart for choosing these teachings of resilience to be shared and for pouring your hearts into the idea of bringing to life the legacy of our resilience heroes.